INTIMACY AS A LENS ON WORK AND MIGRATION

Global Migration and Social Change

Series Editor: **Nando Sigona**, University of Birmingham, UK and **Alexandra Délano Alonso**, The New School, US

This series showcases original research that looks at the nexus between migration, citizenship and social change. The series aims to open up interdisciplinary terrain and to develop new scholarship in migration and refugee studies that is theoretically insightful and innovative, empirically rich and policy engaged.

Scan the code below to discover new and forthcoming titles in the series, or visit:

bristoluniversitypress.co.uk/
global-migration-and-social-change

INTIMACY AS A LENS ON WORK AND MIGRATION

Experiences of Ethnic Performers in Southwest China

Jingyu Mao

First published in Great Britain in 2024 by

Bristol University Press
University of Bristol
1–9 Old Park Hill
Bristol
BS2 8BB
UK
t: +44 (0)117 374 6645
e: bup-info@bristol.ac.uk

Details of international sales and distribution partners are available at bristoluniversitypress.co.uk

© Bristol University Press 2024

British Library Cataloguing in Publication Data
A catalogue record for this book is available from the British Library

ISBN 978-1-5292-2585-3 hardcover
ISBN 978-1-5292-2586-0 ePub
ISBN 978-1-5292-2587-7 ePdf

The right of Jingyu Mao to be identified as author of this work has been asserted by her in accordance with the Copyright, Designs and Patents Act 1988.

All rights reserved: no part of this publication may be reproduced, stored in a retrieval system, or transmitted in any form or by any means, electronic, mechanical, photocopying, recording, or otherwise without the prior permission of Bristol University Press.

Every reasonable effort has been made to obtain permission to reproduce copyrighted material. If, however, anyone knows of an oversight, please contact the publisher.

The statements and opinions contained within this publication are solely those of the author and not of the University of Bristol or Bristol University Press. The University of Bristol and Bristol University Press disclaim responsibility for any injury to persons or property resulting from any material published in this publication.

Bristol University Press works to counter discrimination on grounds of gender, race, disability, age and sexuality.

Cover design: Andrew Corbett
Front cover image: Stocksy/Bo Bo
Bristol University Press use environmentally responsible print partners.
Printed and bound in Great Britain by CPI Group (UK) Ltd, Croydon, CR0 4YY

For my parents Liu Qiong and Mao Baoxiang

Contents

List of Figures		viii
Glossary		ix
About the Author		x
Acknowledgements		xi
Series Preface		xiv
1	Introduction	1
2	Ethnic Performance Work	25
3	Intimate Negotiations along Rural–Urban Borders	51
4	Encountering Ethnicity	74
5	Gendering the Border Struggles	99
6	Conclusion	122
Notes		132
References		133
Index		147

List of Figures

2.1	Performers at Waterfall Restaurant having an early dinner at 4 pm, so that they will be ready to serve dining guests throughout the night	27
2.2	*Bancan* at Forest Park	29
2.3	Ethnic performers under the 'Han gaze'	31
2.4	Service encounters between performers and guests	45

Glossary

Hukou	户口	household registration
Dagong	打工	doing migrant work
Minzu	民族	ethnicity
Shaoshu minzu	少数民族	ethnic minority
Minzu biaoyan	民族表演	ethnic performance
Minzu cun	民族村	ethnic folk villages
Minzu fengqing	民族风情	ethnic flavour
Nongjiale	农家乐	rural tourism
Suzhi	素质	human quality
Bancan	伴餐	accompanying meals
Han	汉族	ethnic Hann
Wa	佤族	ethnic Wa
Hani	哈尼族	ethnic Hani
Lahu	拉祜族	ethnic Lahu
Yi	彝族	ethnic Yi
Dai	傣族	ethnic Dai
Miao	苗族	ethnic Miao
Guanxi	关系	relationship/connection
Pinyin	拼音	romanization of Mandarin
Yanzhi	颜值	appearance value
Zhongguo Meng	中国梦	the China Dream
Nongzhuancheng	农转城	transfer *hukou* from the rural areas to urban areas
Zhengnengliang	正能量	positive energy
Jianshimian	见世面	out to see the world
Hanhua	汉化	Hanification
Ronghe	融合	ethnic assimilation
Fazhan	发展	develop
Jiedai	接待	catering to guests

About the Author

Jingyu Mao is a lecturer in Sociology at the University of Edinburgh. Before joining Edinburgh, she was a postdoctoral research fellow at Bielefeld University and a visiting fellow at the University of Würzburg. Her research interests include migration, work, emotion, intimacy, rural–urban inequality, ethnicity, and gender. Her work has appeared in journals such as *The China Quarterly*, *China Perspectives*, *Emotions and Society*, and *Families, Relationships, and Societies*. She is co-editing two forthcoming special issues for *Global Social Policy* and the *Journal of Political Sociology*.

Acknowledgements

This project would not be possible without the generous supports of my informants, the ethnic performers in Southwest China, who have entrusted me with their personal and emotional stories. I am deeply indebted to their generosity and kindness, and hope this book lived up to their trust.

This book project started in 2015 when I embarked on a life-changing journey to pursue a PhD in Sociology at the University of Edinburgh. I found myself extremely lucky to have the most wonderful supervisors a student could wish for. Professor Mary Holmes provided inspiring and rigorous academic guidance with warmth and a great sense of humour. Dr Sophia Woodman, whose deep care for her students makes me a lucky beneficiary, generously provided food for thought each step of the way. Both Mary and Sophia provided me with thought-provoking intellectual guidance, life-nurturing emotional support, and continued support even after I completed my PhD. They set a very high bar for me and led me to wish to one day become the kind of academics and mentors they are. I feel very blessed to be able to work together with them, and now call them my colleagues and friends. My viva examiners Professor Amy Hanser and Professor Julie Brownlie provided generous and insightful feedback for my thesis, which this book has continued to benefit from. Special thanks go to my Master's dissertation supervisor Dr Carol Wolkowitz, who sparked my academic interests and convinced me that I could dare to pursue a PhD.

I graduated at the height of the COVID-19 pandemic in June 2020 and became unemployed straight away. During the long and challenging days of unemployment, the kind and generous support of my supervisors, mentors, and colleagues kept me going. Dr Ala Sirriyeh, whose insightful and warm mentorship demonstrated great feminist solidarity, became my mentor through the FSA (Feminist Studies Associate) mentoring scheme. Dr Isabelle Darmon always forwarded me job information whenever she saw it, and never hesitated to say yes when I needed help. Dr Tim Pringle and Dr Charlotte Goodburn supported the postdoctoral fellowships I applied for at various points (although without success), making me nevertheless indebted to their generosity. Professor Björn Alpermann and Professor Elena Meyer-Clement, through their jointly led research project, granted me a visiting fellowship in 2021, which became the one thing I could look forward to when I felt most hopeless about an academic career.

In November 2021, I landed my first academic job and joined the Sociology Faculty at Bielefeld University in Germany. Luckily, I soon found myself surrounded by like-minded colleagues and friends. Professor Minh Nguyen always inspired me with her academic rigour, intellectual depth, and deep commitment to marginalized groups. I benefited greatly from her kind and generous mentorship as a junior scholar. Dr Phill Wilcox, the most generous colleague one could ever hope for, has very courageously read and commented on the whole manuscript, alongside helping me to buy a bicycle and coaching me on running. Although I remain a lousy runner, I am deeply indebted to her collegiality and warm friendship. I also had the pleasure to work closely with Ngoc Minh Luong and Yueran Tian in the same ERC team and, other than academic discussions, shared many bowls of pho. Although we often joke about Bielefeld and how it allegedly does not exist according to a conspiracy theory, it remains a place warm in my heart.

My sincere thanks go to my academic friends, whose warm friendships and kind supports make my academic journey much less lonely, and whose intellectual pursuits kept inspiring me in different ways. They are Dr Yan Zhu, Dr Lisa Kalayji, Mr Michael Malzer, Dr Jiazhi Fengjiang, Ms Ruiyao Tian, Dr Kailing Xie, Dr Ling Tang, (very soon to be) Dr Chong Liu, Dr Xiaotian Li, Dr Marie Larsson, and Dr Qing Lin. While working on the PhD thesis, I spent most of my time working from home in London. Therefore, I owe deep gratitude to my dearest friends Qiao Zhao, Melvin Li, Betty Guo, Tanzib Chaudhary, Candice Andrade, and Jason Andrade for making London feel like home. I thank them for their enduring friendship after I moved to Germany and then Edinburgh, and always look forward to having hotpot with them whenever we gather. My friends in China, Xiaoyan Li, Yang Hong, Bin Yan, Yan Yang, and Luling Huang, are constant sources of support, which I am always grateful for.

The editorial team at Bristol University Press provided support each step of the way, which I deeply appreciate. I especially thank Shannon Kneis, Anna Richardson, and Emily Ross for working closely with me on this book. I would also like to thank the constructive and detailed comments I received from the reviewer.

This book received funding at various stages: the Great Britain–China Student Award provided financial support for my PhD. A visiting fellowship through 'Social Worlds: Chinese Cities as Spaces of Worldmaking' funded by the German Federal Ministry of Education and Research (grant no. 01UC2000D) allowed me to work on the manuscript while visiting Wurzburg University in 2021. The time taken to finalize the manuscript was generously funded by the European Research Council project WelfareStruggles (grant no. 803614).

Last, but not the least, I thank my parents Qiong Liu and Baoxiang Bao, whose unfailing love made me the woman I am today. They are always my cheerleaders at the front row, cheering for every little progress I made, and always being there for me when I need it the most. Thank you my dear cat QiuQiu for taking care of me in your own way. I thank my husband Sicheng Ding, who is with me every step of the way. Among a million things to thank Sicheng for, I thank him for cherishing my dream as much as he cherishes his own, if not more.

Some parts of this book have previously appeared elsewhere. I sincerely thank the following publishers which permitted me to use them again in this book:

Mao, J. (2023). Doing ethnicity: multi-layered ethnic scripts in contemporary China. *The China Quarterly*, 1–15. © The Author(s), 2023. Published by Cambridge University Press on behalf of SOAS University of London.

Mao, J. (2023). Bringing emotional reflexivity and emotional regime to understanding 'the hukou puzzle' in contemporary China. *Emotions and Society*. Bristol University Press. Retrieved November 17, 2023, from https://doi.org/10.1332/263169021X16731871958851

Mao, J. (2021). Bordering work and personal life: using 'the multiplication of labour' to understand ethnic performers' work in Southwest China. *China Perspectives,* 124: 9–18.

Series Preface

Jingyu Mao's book, *Intimacy as a Lens on Work and Migration: Experiences of Ethnic Performers in Southwest China,* is an essential book to understand the impact of the *hukou* registration system in the everyday lives of internal migrants in China. Through an intimate look at the experiences of ethnic performers who migrate from rural to urban areas in search for better job opportunities, Mao offers new insights into the role of emotions, not only in the process of internal migration within the restrictions of the *hukou* system, but in the lived experiences of men and women who, in the process of intra provincial migration, encounter bordering processes related to ethnicity, gender and sexuality.

As part of the Global Migration and Social Change series, this book joins our efforts to bring forward original theoretical and methodological approaches to the study of migration. In particular, Mao's book expands our understanding of internal migration dynamics in China, specifically in the Southwest area of the country, which has so far been underexplored. This subregional and small-city focus also sheds light on labour dynamics that go beyond the common understanding of internal migration in the context of manufacturing work, showing instead the dynamics of labour within the tourism industry, particularly related to ethnic performers, which reveal aspects of intimate relationships, gender, sexuality and ethnicity that have so far not been centred in other existing accounts of Chinese migration.

One of the largest population movements in human history, internal migration in China is estimated to include 295 million people in 2022. The *hukou* regime, a household registration system which divides the population into 'rural' and 'urban' populations, registers people according to their place of birth, and which was initially established to control geographic mobility, creates restrictions that put millions of people in vulnerable positions when they are forced to move in search of opportunity. As Mao explains, the system is multi-layered and has become an integral part of China's economic and political system and social stratification, as it limits people's access to certain labour opportunities, public housing and welfare systems.

Intimacy as a Lens on Work and Migration shows how, despite recent reforms, the system continues to put migrants in precarious positions. With a focus on a small city and through an 'intimacy lens' methodology, the book centers the experiences of young people who are ethnic minorities according to official registrations, and who, despite not feeling very strongly attached to their ethnic identities, make sense of them in a context of internal displacement, particularly in a context where their ethnicity is a segregating factor in the labour market. Beyond its important contribution to migration studies, this work yields important insights in understanding how power and inequalities work in contemporary China.

Alexandra Délano Alonso and Nando Sigona

1

Introduction

If you visit 'Green City' in Yunnan Province, Southwest China (I have anonymized the name of the city), you will probably be advised by local people or tourist guidebooks to go and see local ethnic performance shows as part of your trip. Indeed, the moment that you arrive at the regional airport you will see posters featuring ethnic minority people, most of whom are young women dressed in colourful minority costumes, smiling warmly and singing passionately against a backdrop of mountain views. The posters usually say something like 'Be ready to be welcomed by our most heart-warmingly hospitable ethnic minority people', or 'Be ready to have a taste of our most authentic ethnic culture'. These posters are visible and prevalent among the numerous advertisements and billboards in Green City, which is striving to turn itself into a popular tourist destination.

It used to be the case that you had to go to formal theatres or to performance stages at tourist sites in order to watch ethnic performances. But in recent years you have been able to do that at your dining table if you visit certain restaurants in Green City. This normally involves ethnic minority people singing and dancing in front of your table, and making toasts to you in their traditional way. As someone who grew up in Green City, I initially found the recently emerged forms of ethnic performances interesting. I had visited these restaurants and tourist sites as a customer before I began my research and was impressed by some of their performances. But after I tried to see ethnic performances through the performers' points of view through conducting this research, I started to understand it in drastically different ways.

In 2016, as I started doing fieldwork in one of the restaurants which features ethnic performances – I call it Waterfall Restaurant– I sat down with a man named Jun for an interview. Jun is one of the ethnic performers from the group of people that this book focuses on. Dressed in a colourful minority costume, Jun explained to me his decision to become an ethnic performer. "I'm tired of working like a robot everyday … Yes, that's how I feel when I work in that factory in Guangdong; I feel like I'm a robot when I sit on the assembly line every day and every hour." For Jun, escaping boring and repressive factory work was one of the most important reasons that he decided to come back to his home province and find work in Green City, which is not far from the rural village that he comes from. Being a Lahu, which is one of the 55 groups of ethnic minorities in China, he learnt from his friends' experiences that he could take up work as an ethnic performer, and that is how he started to work as a performer/waiter in Waterfall Restaurant. Ironically, by escaping boring factory work, Jun encountered perhaps even greater workplace challenges in the field of service work and ethnic performance.

This book details the experiences of ethnic performers like Jun, who are rural–urban migrants, and many of whom are from ethnic minority backgrounds. At work, ethnic performers dress in colourful minority costumes, and perform ethnic songs and dances at venues such as restaurants and tourist sites. As rural–urban migrants, many of them are intra-provincial migrants from adjacent villages, of which the distance from Green City ranges from a half an hour to four hours' drive. Many of them have never migrated outside the province, lacking the resources and networks to migrate that far away. Some of them have chosen to move to a nearby town or city to work, for various reasons relating to family, personal preference, and so on. Regardless of how far they move, migrant performers face challenges that are lived in and through their intimate lives. As this book elucidates, ethnic performance becomes a site of encounter where minority, rural, feminized service providers interact with Han, urban, masculinized customers, and such physical proximity renders their social distance even more significant. It is also an important site where performers encounter various bordering processes, most notably related to rural–urban migration, ethnicity, and gender. Here, I refer bordering as the different processes of making boundaries and drawing distinctions, and how territorial borders constantly intersect with the symbolic, cultural, and bureaucratic ones to regulate labour and mobility, leading to different forms of inclusion and exclusion. This book explores the intimate consequences of such border encounters which relate to performers' emotions, sense of self, and relationships, and uses these intimate negotiations as starting point of inquiry to understand broader processes of inequalities – an approach that I call 'intimacy as lens'. This introductory chapter contextualizes who migrant performers are and why their experiences are worth researching, provides a theoretical framework of the book, utilizing the concepts of intimacy as a lens and border encounters, and finally provides a brief outline of the chapters that follow. It demonstrates how ethnic performers' experiences of work and migration becomes a fruitful site to unpack the multi-layered and entangled inequalities of the rural–urban divide, ethnicity, and gender, and how the lens of intimacy yields important insights in understanding how power and inequalities work in contemporary China.

Researching 'untypical migrants': ethnic migrant performers in Southwest China

The ethnic migrant performers upon whom this research focuses are all rural–urban migrants who have moved from rural villages to work and live in urban areas. Yet their migration is somehow different from the classic rural–urban trajectory and, as ethnic minority migrants who move within a province to a small-scale city and who undertake service work, their experiences have received less scholarly attention. Researching such 'untypical migrants' enables a more nuanced understanding of the heterogeneity of migrant subjectivities and experiences.

Being one of the largest population movements in human history, rural–urban migration in China has been a major force in shaping Chinese society for the last four decades. The number of migrants has been rising since the 1980s, reaching 295 million in 2022 according to national census data (National Bureau of Statistics, 2023). Migrants are motivated to move to cities for various reasons, including economic reasons, family reasons, and a desire to see the outside world. Among these reasons, the huge equality gap between the rural and the urban is the fundamental reason that motivates millions of migrants to find work in the city. This does not only refer to the large income gap between the rural and urban populations, but also to the unequal access to various social resources such as education, pensions, and health care. Just like the unequal global development that has pushed migrant men and women from the Global South to seek work in the Global North, migration to the cities has become the Chinese migrants' personal solution to a public problem (Ehrenreich and Hochschild, 2003).

Numerous studies have sought to theorize this significant phenomenon, from its political and economic impact on Chinese society to the life stories of the migrants involved in this huge movement. Many debates about China's domestic migration centre on the *hukou* regime: the household registration system which divides the population into 'rural' and 'urban' populations, and registers people according to their place of birth. Established in 1958, *hukou* was initially intended to control geographic mobility. However, its function has proven to be multi-layered, and it has become an integral part of China's economic and political system and social stratification. *Hukou* functions in a way similar to Castles's (1995) depiction of 'differential exclusion', which ensures that migrants are incorporated into certain areas of society (most prominently labour markets) but are denied access to others – such as welfare systems. Without *hukou* to guarantee access to certain welfare provisions, public housing, and particular jobs in cities, migrants from rural areas have become marginalized as 'second class citizens' (Solinger, 1999; Chan, 2010). Despite several waves of reforms which have loosened the restrictions of *hukou*, especially in small- to medium-sized cities, *hukou* continues to put migrant workers in a 'permanent position of legal and economic instability and vulnerability' (Nyíri, 2010: 19; Dong and Goodburn, 2020; Lin and Mao, 2022a).

With the initial plan to conduct research on migrant workers in China, I did not intend to do this research in Green City, planning instead to do it in Shenzhen – a city in the Pearl River Delta which absorbs the largest number of rural–urban migrants in China. The choice of city was based on my understanding of migrant workers, who move from western, inland provinces to work in factories in eastern, coastal cities, or big cities such as Beijing or Shanghai, which is based on the major pattern of rural–urban migration in China, as supported by statistics (Liang and Ma, 2014). My understanding was also shaped by existing literature, which tends to depict a rather homogenous picture of migrant workers working in the factories, mostly notably in the Pearl River Delta (see, for example, Lee, 1998; Pun, 2005; Chan et al, 2020). Such a picture was so ingrained in my mind that when I thought about potential informants for this research, my immediate inclination was to look for factory workers in Shenzhen.

However, I changed my initial plan due to the lack of networks and resources to facilitate the research in Shenzhen. Besides such practical considerations, a reassessment of my research plan drew my attention to a less high-profile city, for which migrant labour is crucial for its functioning yet tends to go under the scholarly radar – my hometown, Green City, a small-scale city in Yunnan Province, Southwest China. It is by no means a popular destination for rural–urban migrants, and it is mostly people from adjacent rural villages who choose to find work there. However, focusing on such an 'ordinary city' (Robinson, 2013) had the potential to yield insights that might have been overlooked by only focusing on the major migrant cities. While most migration literature is about migrants who migrate to eastern and coastal cities, relatively little material draws attention to migration to and within western China, despite the trend that more capital and investments are moving to western and inland China. There is also little research about people who move within their home province, and who move to small- to medium-sized cities, although numbers of such migrants have been rising rapidly in recent years (Liang et al, 2014; Liang, 2016). A report on migrant workers shows that 'Chinese workers appear to be increasingly reluctant to migrate far away from their hometowns ... and inter-provincial migrants are also dropping' (Made in China Journal, 2017). In 2015, 54.1 per cent of China's rural–urban migrants were intra-provincial migrants, outnumbering the migrants who moved to other provinces (Su et al, 2018). Meanwhile, several waves of *hukou* reforms, with the most recent one announced in

2014, place small- and medium-sized cities (with populations of less than 500,000) at the forefront of the change. *Hukou* restrictions become more relaxed in smaller cities, and migrant are theoretically allowed to transfer their *hukou* from rural homes to cities if they are willing to do so (Chen and Fan, 2016; Zhang, 2018). This book brings new perspectives to understanding migrants' experiences of being at the forefront of *hukou* reform, as they navigate a *hukou* system which appears to be loosening its control over migrants, yet continues to play a significant role in 'bordering' migration in China (Johnson, 2017). All these changes and literature gaps point to the value of studying migrants who move from a rural area to a small-sized city within the region of Southwest China.

My interest in knowing more about rural–urban migrants' lives, ironically, was co-existent with my ignorance about the migrant workers whose labour I rely upon as a city dweller. Service workers in Green City are mostly rural–urban migrants, but I did not seem to realize this until I undertook my research, as their presence and work formerly seemed invisible to me. At that time, the most 'visible' group of rural–urban migrants was made up of the ethnic performers that I had met as a customer in previous years – this also points to how visible the rural origins of performers are to outsiders, as rurality and ethnicity intertwine in particular ways in China. It also shows how differences are constantly marked and reinforced through performers' everyday work, and which all became important themes to explore in this book.

Another factor that motivated me to do this research is my personal interest in knowing more about the younger generation of ethnic minority people in China. While the Han majority constitutes 91.51 per cent of China's population, 55 groups of ethnic minorities comprise the remaining 8.49 per cent according to official registrations. I myself am officially registered as Hani, one of the minority groups. As someone who is ethnic minority according to official registration, I am expected by others to say something about my culture once they learn that I am a Hani. I sometimes feel guilty or ashamed of not being able to say something meaningful about Hani culture or identity, with which I have long since lost the connection. Sometimes I have even been a bit surprised by the questions people ask me – "Do you sing ethnic songs and dance during holidays?" or "Do you wear ethnic costumes during special occasions?" The fact that people impose 'the common knowledge' about ethnic minorities in China when they encounter me as an individual is both telling and sociologically interesting. What is missing from such common knowledge or stereotypical imaginings is how young people who are ethnic minorities according to official registrations, but who may not feel very strongly attached to their ethnic identities, make sense of them. Even literature about ethnic minority people in China does not address this point adequately. The available movies, books, and even literature tend to depict ethnic minority people as living in remote mountainous areas and practising distinct cultural rituals and ways of living which are not necessarily compatible with urban, modern ways of life. Such discrepancies between official designation and people's lived experiences of ethnicity became a major theme for this book, as it is not just my personal problem but a public concern that speaks to many of my informants, as I later found out through fieldwork.

There are also few pieces of literature focusing on ethnic minority people who are on the move. The migrant performers this book focuses on come from different ethnic backgrounds, including but not limited to Dai, Lahu, Wa, and Hani, which are among the 55 state-recognized ethnic groups. These officially defined *minzu* (ethnic) categories are based on the Ethnic Classification Project carried out by the CCP (Chinese Communist Party) in the 1950s, which recognized the 55 groups from 400 groups that filed applications for recognition. This project is problematic in many ways, since it undermined the rights and interests of some ethnic groups in order to maintain a unified picture of the People's Republic of China (PRC) (Mullaney, 2011; Zang, 2015). Despite immense efforts to develop economies in ethnic minority regions and fruitful achievements in raising the living standards of ethnic minority people, the economic gap between the Han group and ethnic minority groups has been widening alarmingly since the 1980s market reforms (Zang, 2015). Together with the widening gap between rural and urban areas, out-migration is increasingly common among ethnic minority people in rural areas.

However, in discussions of China's rural–urban migration, the experiences of ethnic minority migrants are largely unexplored, with a few exceptions that try to bring ethnicity into the discussion (see, for example, Iredale et al, 2001; Howell and Fan, 2011; Ma, 2019). Therefore, we have little understanding of how ethnic minority migrants' experiences may differ from their Han counterparts, and whether ethnicity plays an important role in shaping migrants' work and life experiences. The lack of discussion about ethnicity in migration studies in China might be because of the difficulty of obtaining migration data that incorporate ethnicity, and also possibly the assumption that ethnicity plays a small role in migration journeys (Howell and Fan, 2011). Chinese authorities also discourage discussions of migration or other social issues through the lens of ethnicity, promoting instead an ideology of assimilation (see, for example, Ma, 2007) – an issue to which I will return in Chapter 4. Ethnic minorities are stereotypically believed to be immobile and stay in remote and mountainous areas. However, despite the fact that the majority of rural–urban migrants are Han, there is also a considerable proportion of rural–urban migrants who come from ethnic minority backgrounds, and whose experiences of migration cannot be captured by large-scale surveys, as has tended to be the case in studies so far

(Gustafsson and Yang, 2015; Howell et al, 2020). Their voices deserve to be better recognized in understanding how ethnicity shapes their migration experiences. Meanwhile, ethnicity has become a segregating factor in the labour market, with ethnic minority people affected more by urban labour market declines then their Han counterparts (Maurer-Fazio et al, 2007), which means that there are even fewer job opportunities for ethnic minority migrants in the city. Some of the ethnic minority migrants consequently have had to take up jobs with distinctive ethnic cultural characterizations, among which ethnic tourism roles have become an option.

When focusing on the case of ethnic performers, it is important to recognize the unique dynamic of their work, which, as will be demonstrated in Chapter 2, is a form of interactive service work (Leidner, 1991). It embodies different dynamics than factory work, which is the focus of the majority of research about migrant workers in China (Swider, 2017). A recent transformation in the labour market has witnessed an increasing number of migrant workers working in the service industry, while migrants employed in manufacturing work has fallen dramatically in recent years (China Labour Bulletin, 2019). Statistics show that factories in China have been facing increasingly severe labour shortages since 2008, while more and more migrant workers have chosen to work in the service sector rather than the manufacturing sector (Choi and Peng, 2015; Shen, 2019). This has not been sufficiently discussed in the migration literature. Whereas producers working in factories usually do not have direct contact with the consumers of their labour, people who work in the frontline of service jobs have close proximity to the consumers that they are serving. Such physical proximity may render their social distance more prominent and visible. Therefore, the changing dynamics of migrants' work need further exploring.

Existing research on migrant workers in the service sector points to how work has become an important site for workers' negotiations around gender, emotions, bodies, and sexualities (Zheng, 2007; Hanser, 2008; Otis, 2011; Shen, 2019). While the day-to-day encounter between service providers and customers produces social distinctions, and shapes the subjectivity of service workers, it also becomes an important site to understand the intersecting inequalities in China. So far, gender is the most prominent focus in the study of service work in China. Indeed, the majority of the service workers in this research are female, and ethnic performance relies heavily on migrant women's gendered and sexualized labour, which is further complicated and coloured by the issue of ethnicity (see Chapter 5). However, gender is not the only, nor the most important, lens to understand service work in this research since ethnic performance as a unique form of service work is deeply shaped by cultural and political assumptions of ethnicity. As migrants rely on performing a certain version of their own ethnicity for an audience of Han tourists, such daily encounters of ethnicity not only engender the reflexivity of their ethnic identity, but also push them to work on their ethnic selves in certain ways in order to be valuable in the labour market. This is a process that is filled with ambivalences and emotional struggles. Yet, with the representations of ethnic performance being prevalent in many cultural and political spheres in China, performers' own voices are usually silenced and overlooked.

The prevalent ethnic performance and the silenced performers

Ethnic performance (*minzu biaoyan*), which usually involves the performance of ethnic songs and dances by people dressed in colourful minority clothes, is prevalent in many cultural spheres in China. As Dru Gladney (1994: 95) succinctly noted: '[o]ne cannot be exposed to China without being confronted by its colourful minorities. They sing, they dance, they twirl, they whirl. Most of all they smile, showing their happiness to be part of the motherland.' In the early socialist period of the PRC, ethnic performance was actively incorporated into the state-building project, showcasing minority people as important actors in the building of a socialist China, thereby strengthen the image of China as a unified and harmonious society (Wilcox, 2016). More recently, in the annual *Spring Festival Gala* – the show that most Chinese families watch during the Spring Festivals, and the most watched television programme in the world – there will always be performances of ethnic songs and dances with people dressed in colourful minority costumes, showcasing that they are part of the big Chinese nation-family. Such images also proliferate in textbooks for elementary school students, where songs and dances have become 'the most popular means of representing ethnic minorities in the textbooks' (Chu, 2015: 477). In fact, when I undertook participant observation at tourist sites featuring ethnic performance, I often heard audiences comment impressively on how they had finally got to see the real ethnic minority people that they had only seen before in elementary textbooks. Indeed, despite its indulgence in stereotypes, ethnic performance becomes an important way for many Han Chinese to get to know about ethnic minority people. Such essentialized ways of representing ethnic minority people are also prevalent in tourism spheres. For example, many cities in China have so-called 'ethnic folk villages' (*minzu cun*), where ethnic performances are showcased for mostly Han audiences (see Yang, 2011). In recent years, aligning with the state project of poverty alleviation and rural revitalization, more and more rural villages are incorporating ethnic performance in an effort to turn themselves into tourist sites in order to 'escape poverty' and develop the local economy (Chio, 2014; Rautio, 2021). Ethnic tourism has also been incorporated into many other scenic tourist sites in China, where minority people are depicted as naturally good at singing and dancing, closer to nature than the Han, and primitive yet exotic. This reflects what Louisa Schein (2000) critically calls 'internal orientalism' in China, through which Western representations of 'Eastern' 'Others' (Said, 1978) are readily translated into the Chinese, multi-ethnic context, through which ethnic minorities are essentialized as ethnic Others within their own nation.

The increasing popularity of ethnic performance in commercialized settings should also be understood in relation to the changing landscape of consumption and service work in China. The service sector barely existed in the socialist era of Chinese reform 40 years ago, but by 2018 it accounted for 52.2 per cent of China's gross domestic product (GDP). It has become 'a new engine for economic growth' in China (China Daily, 2019), and although the inequality among different social groups is expanding drastically at the same time (Pun, 2003; Davis, 2005), urban residents in China are witnessing a consumer revolution: new forms of entertainment and consumption are expanding; it is common for more and more urbanites to patronize restaurants; and new ideas keep burgeoning to attract the attention of consumers, including a vast number of *nongjiale* (rural tourism) restaurants (Park, 2014), which seek to provide a nostalgic vision of dining for urban people who are detached from rural ways of living. At the same time, tourism is also becoming more and more affordable for many Chinese citizens, while tourism itself becomes a way for urban middle-class people to assert their privilege and gain cultural capital (Walsh and Swain, 2004; Nyíri, 2010).

The burgeoning commercialization of ethnic performance should also be understood in relation to local conditions. Yunnan Province, where Green City is situated, is one of the most impoverished provinces in China. Promoting ethnic tourism therefore becomes an important way for local government to develop the economy and, to borrow government language, '[lift] itself out of the poverty'. Therefore, the development and promotion of ethnic performance has both economic and political meanings. When ethnic performances are closely tied to ethnic tourism, promoting economic growth and poverty alleviation, local government officials actively seek to bring a 'cultural revival' to the local ethnic culture (Yang and Wall, 2008; McCarthy, 2011). Stories in the mass media proliferate about how ethnic minorities transform themselves from being part of a backward society to being part of a new socialist era, and one Lahu village is often used as an example to showcase its successful reliance on an ethnic cultural revival to 'escape poverty'.

It is in such a context that commercialized ethnic performances have emerged, and they are expanding rapidly. Singing songs and dancing are rituals for certain minority groups on special occasions, at festivals, or as part of their everyday lives (see, for example, Du, 2008). However, under the context of commercialization, what is performed is drastically different from its original form, as it is reconstructed for the purpose of ethnic tourism. It therefore takes on a different meaning from its original one. For example, courtship songs used to be part of the important rituals undertaken before proposing marriage in Lahu villages. In a society where the public manifestation of intimacy and love is strictly controlled, singing courtship songs is one of the occasions when such public expressions of intimacy become legitimate (Du, 2008). However, when such love songs are taken out of their context and performed in front of audiences and tourists, they lose their original meanings. If you searched 'minority toasting' in Chinese on the internet today, you would see all kinds of photos showcasing what it is like to have minority people singing and dancing around your dining table and toasting guests in ways that are supposed to be characteristic of minority cultures. Consequently, it is easy to see how such labour tends to rely on the gendered and sexualized labour of young women (see Chapter 5), and offers an essentialized way to represent ethnic cultures.

While ethnic performances in commercial settings have gained in popularity, little research has focused on the people who undertake this form of labour. Ethnic tourism literature tends to focus on the 'representation' or the cultural meanings of ethnic tourism (see, for example, Walsh and Swain, 2004; Yang, 2011), as well as the ways that ethnic tourism shapes local economic and social conditions (see, for example, Hillman, 2003; Yang and Wall, 2008). Less talked about is how ethnic tourism impacts on the individuals who participate in it (but see Schein, 1997; Li, 2003; Walsh, 2005; Bai, 2007). In other words, the personal voices and experiences of people who participate in ethnic tourism – like the ethnic performers in this research – are rarely regarded as the centre of the focus. Also, while most of this research focuses on local people who engage in ethnic tourism, it neglects non-local migrants who take part and neglects the various ways their migrant status intersects with this work, which may further marginalize them.

Nevertheless, one important finding from the ethnic tourism literature is the ways that participating in such work shapes people's understandings of the meaning of ethnicity. 'The daily reminder of ethnicity' at work pushes people to renegotiate their understandings of ethnicity, as it has become an issue that they have to confront on a daily basis (Li, 2003; Bai, 2007: 257). However, the emphasis of ethnic tourism literature tends to be on the separation between the tourist sphere and everyday life (see, for example, Bai, 2007). In other words, this literature tends to suggest that it is people's ability to separate work and life, or to put a distance between their real self and their working self, which affords them leverage in negotiating the fluidity of ethnicity. For example, research shows that Bai people who participate in local tourism could choose the aspect of ethnic identification which is beneficial for them, and use it towards their own gain (Bai, 2007). Another example is how Dai women who engage in the tourism business have to learn how to actively play upon tourists' fantasies of ethnic minority women in order to be successful. They do so by using different strategies to package Dai culture as a desirable commodity and 'consciously draw a line between a staged "primitive/exotic" self and a "modern" self in contemporary village life' (Li, 2003: 55). The underlying assumption is that people can successfully separate the 'on-stage' self and 'off-stage' self, and therefore can return to their own ways of being ethnic when the tourists depart. While it is true that people can use different strategies to navigate the work landscape in which different assumptions about being ethnic proliferate, such frameworks neglect the ways in which participating in ethnic tourism can have a more profound influence on the individuals involved. Assuming people could successfully put a distance between their work self and 'real self' also neglects the emotional consequences of the daily encounter of ethnicity, and how work in turn shapes subjectivities. This book demonstrates how working as an ethnic performer has a more profound impact on people's sense of self outside the sphere of work. Some performers work on their ethnic selves in ways that are encouraged by the state and market in order to gain more employment opportunities and potentially move up the social ladder (see Chapter 4). The book seeks to gain a deeper understanding of the ways in which work, migration, and personal life intersect in the case of ethnic performers. Working as an ethnic performer has a profound impact on one's emotions and sense of self, as work is a crucial 'site of encounter' through which performers not only have close interactions with guests, but also encounter different bordering processes, most notably in relation to the rural–urban divide, ethnicity, and gender.

Border encounters through migration and work

Unlike working in factories, which is the focus of the majority of work on migrant workers in China, ethnic performance is a site where performers and guests encounter each other in a physically close manner. The unique dynamics of ethnic performance means that they involve 'service encounters' between customers and service providers (Hanser, 2008). As minority, rural, feminized service providers interact with Han, urban, masculinized customers, such physical proximity may render their social distance even greater. Meanwhile, not all strangers are created equal, as some are 'designated as *stranger than other others*' due to the historical legacies that fix certain bodies as 'the Other' (Ahmed, 2013: 6; emphasis in original). A similar point has been made on how some bodies become the markers of strangeness and otherness. In a piece of research on how Chinese men encounter Vietnam through the bodies of Vietnamese sex workers in a city on the Viet-China border, Grillot and Zhang (2016: 146) argue how the figure of Vietnamese women sex workers become 'a boundary marker that signals an "otherness" and unpredictability characteristic of cross-border encounters'. In the context of ethnic performance, Han customers encounter the imagined otherness of ethnic minorities through the embodied and emotional work of ethnic performers, especially female performers. These encounters, although mostly fleeting, have a profound influence on performers' lives, especially the intimate spheres including their emotions, sense of self, and relationships with others. Hence, such encounters not only refer to how people from different social backgrounds interact with each other in a physically close manner in the service context, they also address how ethnic performance becomes a key site where different bordering processes proliferate to regulate labour and migration.

In understanding how performers encounter different bordering processes through their work and migration, this book follows *Border as Method* (Mezzadra and Neilson, 2013) in understanding bordering as the processes of making boundaries and drawing distinctions, which overlap territorial borders (such as rural and urban) with their non-territorial (such as symbolic, cultural, and cognitive) forms in producing different types of inclusion and exclusions (see also Mao, 2021). For example, in China, the bordering between the rural and urban relies not only on the territorial boundaries between the two, it also relies on the aforementioned mechanism of *hukou* in making borders within the national territorial boundary of the state (Johnson, 2017). Moreover, the symbolic and cultural dimensions of bordering are also significant in designating different meanings to the rural (for example, as backward and in need of constant improvement) and the urban (for example, as modern and the embodiment of progress). Together, these territorial, bureaucratic, symbolic, and cultural elements all constitute the bordering between the rural and urban, and it is something ethnic performers need to constantly grapple with through their everyday work and migration experiences (see Chapter 3). Similar bordering processes also occur along the divisions of the Han and the minority, masculinity, and femininity, which are all important themes to be explored in the following chapters. This book also pays special attention to the agentive power of borders in producing and shaping subjectivities. This means that it will explore the many intimate, emotional, and personal consequences for these ethnic performers of having to encounter borders on a daily basis. In understanding border encounters as always emotional, intimate, and personal, this book further proposes the framework of 'intimacy as a lens' to 'use micro-scale everyday bordering practices to both conceptualize and visualize what borders are at a more general level' (Yuval-Davis, 2013: 16).

Intimacy as a lens

'Intimacy as a lens' refers to how a series of 'private' negotiations that people make regarding their emotions, sense of self, and relationships could become an effective tool in understanding broader social inequalities. It means commencing with the personal realm and using that as a starting point of social inquiry. This, on the one hand, echoes what Wanning Sun (2023), in studying social inequalities in China, calls 'the intimate turn', which elucidates the intimate consequences of inequality and considers how individuals feel such inequalities emotionally through their private lives, such as love and romantic relationships. On the other hand, intimacy as a lens not only focuses on the *consequences* of inequality, but also uses intimacy as a *means* to study social inequality. In this way, intimacy becomes an epistemological and methodological device through which the nature of social inequality, and the mechanisms through which it comes into power, can be explored more thoroughly.

While issues of the rural–urban divide and ethnicity tend to be discussed from macro perspectives in China (see, however, the notable examples of Choi and Peng, 2016; Sun, 2023), intimacy as a lens reveals how starting from 'the personal' could reveals insights that are often neglected otherwise. For instance, starting from performers' ambivalence over whether or not they are 'authentic' ethnic minorities, Chapter 4 offers novel perspectives in understanding the politics of ethnicity in contemporary China, which regards ethnicity as something people do, and recognizing the multi-layered 'ethnic scripts' that shape people's doing of ethnicity. The emotion of ambivalence is a subtle one, which can be easily neglected by social theorists on ethnicity. Yet intimacy as a lens takes these micro and intimate concerns seriously and acts as a fruitful tool to understand broader social and cultural forces at play in constituting multi-layered inequalities which, in turn, shapes individuals' intimate spheres.

Intimacy as a lens is built upon two strands of sociological theory: the sociology of personal life (Smart, 2007; May, 2011) and sociology of intimacy (Jamieson, 1999, 2011). The sociology of personal life is a move away from what has traditionally been designated as the sociology of family and kinship, as it incorporates other relationships and areas of life that are crucial for individuals, and provides new ways of thinking about personhood and the blurring boundaries between the public and the private (Smart, 2007). It seeks to ask, 'what is sociological about personal life, that is, what individual people's personal lives say about society more generally' (May, 2011: 2).

Two insights from the sociology of personal life are particularly useful in understanding ethnic performers' experiences. Firstly, the personal life approach emphasizes how the personal is always relational, which means that people's sense of self is 'constructed *in relationships with* others, and *in relation* to others and to social norms' (May, 2011: 7; emphasis in original). It therefore challenges the 'individualization thesis' (Giddens, 1991; Beck, 1992; Beck and Beck-Gernsheim, 1995), which assumes that people in modernity are autonomous, with all kinds of free choices, disembedded from their historical and cultural contexts, and disconnected from webs of relationships. Such insight is particularly important in the context of China, where the project of individualization remains an ambition rather than an achieved reality (Wang and Nehring, 2014), especially when the authoritarian state still plays a strong role in shaping the ideals of a moral person, and often ties that closely with the intimate spheres (Xie, 2021). The following chapters will demonstrate how migrant performers keep 'working' on themselves in ways that accord with the social and cultural ideals of a respectable and valuable personhood (Skeggs, 1997, 2011), and exercise their emotional reflexivity in relational ways, with considerations of their family and significant others.

The second insight from the personal life approach is to treat different spheres of life as not separate areas, but as closely interconnected (May, 2011). Such 'connectedness' suggests that we do not experience our lives in segregated spheres as defined by, for example, the sociology of work or the sociology of migration (May, 2011). Our personal lives do not end once we step into 'public' spaces. Meanwhile, what we experience in the 'public' sphere also in turn shapes our 'personal' lives. Indeed, the intersection between work and personal life remains an under-theorized topic in sociology (Smart, 2007), despite the personal life approach's endeavours to address such connectedness. As an intervention, this book points to how the borders that contain work and personal lives are no longer stable, since what performers experience at work also has a profound impact on their personal lives outside the work sphere. Such entanglement also calls into question the boundaries that demarcate the public and the personal.

Despite efforts to attend to a wider range of relationships, much literature on personal life remains centred on family relationships. Family relationships are not the main focus of this research, as it is more concerned with people's intimate experiences of encountering different bordering processes through work and migration. Also, without specifically defined boundaries regarding what constitutes 'personal life', which is also arguably one of the strengths of 'personal life' as a framework, this framework is too broad in practical theorization – in a sense, every aspect of life can constitute one's personal life. Therefore, while borrowing important insights from 'personal life', 'intimacy as a lens' further narrows down its focus to make its operation more practical.

While intimacy as a concept in sociology usually refers to the quality of closeness in relationships (Jamieson, 1999, 2011), this research uses this concept in more than one way and explores how it can be used as a theoretical and methodological tool to explore broader social structures. Hence, the lens of intimacy means starting from the intimate realm and working from there to understand broader social issues. More specifically, by focusing on a series of intimate negotiations people have regarding their emotions, sense of self, and relationships, this approach seeks to use micro-scale negotiations to illuminate the social forces at work. While numerous pieces of research have firmly established that 'the personal is political', the lens of intimacy allows a more systematic approach in exploring how 'the social' can be better understood by taking 'the personal' seriously.

The lens of intimacy departs from and contributes to existing theories of personal life and intimacy in the following ways: firstly, while both theories of personal life and intimacy recognize the important role emotions play in shaping relationships and social lives, emotions are nonetheless often theorized in relation to family lives and personal relationships. Without diminishing the importance of such a focus, it would be beneficial to theorize emotions without confining them to the relationship spheres. This book explores performers' emotions in relation to the migration regime (Chapter 3), as well as in relation to the state-designated categories of ethnicity (Chapter 4). It recognizes how it is emotionally challenging to work on the frontier of service work, and having to constantly interact with customers who hold different stereotypes and gendered expectations toward the performers (Chapter 2 and Chapter 5). Further, rather than treating emotions as the consequences of migration and work, this approach further asks what emotions do, and what can be revealed by focusing on them. It seeks to situate individuals' emotions in relation to the broader 'emotional regime' – the way that different social and historical contexts shape people's emotional expressions (Reddy, 2001). Several literatures point out how 'positive energy' and 'happiness' discourses are crucial in constituting China's contemporary emotional regime (Kleinman, 2011; Hird, 2018; Wielander, 2018; Wielander and Hird, 2018; Mao, 2023b). The use of emotions has also been incorporated in the state's techniques of governance, as the term 'therapeutic governance' vividly describes how the state governs through managing people's emotions, most prominently through discourses about 'happiness' (Yang, 2014). Using intimacy as a lens entails bringing an emotionally informed approach to the study of social inequalities. It means asking questions such as what inequalities feel like to people (see, for example, Skeggs, 1997, 2011; Sun, 2023), and how people's feelings and emotions, in turn, reveal the ways power and inequalities work.

Secondly, in thinking about personhood, this approach emphasizes the relational aspect of self-making, especially how people work on their personhood in relation to socio-cultural norms, which define 'valuable personhood' in various ways (Skeggs, 2011). Theories about personhood in China effectively capture the changing landscape of self-making under the rapidly changing social and moral context (see, for example, Yan, Y., 2003; Rofel, 2007; Hoffman, 2010; Yan, 2010). The emergence of a sense of the individual and a desire to see the outside world is regarded as a major landmark in China's individualization process (Yan, Y., 2003; Yan, 2010). Rural–urban migrants were actually used as an example to illustrate the individualization process in China, as migrants

> had to deal with their work and life in the cities as individuals, away from both home and family ... In other words, mobility serves as an important agent of transformation as it enables disembedment, making it possible for the individual to break out of the shadow of the various sorts of collectives. (Yan, 2010: 497)

At the same time, marketization and increasing competition nurtured what Rose calls the 'enterprising self', which means that individuals keep managing their selves as if they are enterprises (Rose, 1992). The state also plays a strong role in shaping the 'enterprising self', as young Chinese professionals actively incorporate patriotism into their senses of self (Hoffman, 2010). Meanwhile, neoliberalism and globalization in the Chinese context encourage 'the desiring self', in which individuals' aspirations, needs, and longings are closely related to consumption, sexuality, and cosmopolitanism (Rofel, 2007). However, some of these theories risk the same trap of the 'individualization thesis' in the West, which neglects the ways that self-making is also relational and less free-floating than assumed. Existing research has also demonstrated that individualism remains an ambition rather than an achieved reality in China, as the state and a series of institutionalized inequalities still permeates individuals' intimate lives in influential ways (Wang and Nehring, 2014).

In China, the discourse of *suzhi* plays a crucial role in understanding personhood. *Suzhi* is generally translated into 'human quality', which is used in the various governing processes, and is also widely used in daily life (Kipnis, 2006). *Suzhi* discourse was often related to neoliberal governmentality, since they share the similar deployment of value coding which 'inscribes, measures, and mobilises human subjectivity as the powerhouse for productivity and development' (Yan, H., 2003: 497). In that sense, some people are regarded as embodying high *suzhi*, while others are deemed as embodying low *suzhi* – rural–urban migrants and ethnic minority people are often related with the latter (see, for example, Friedman, 2006; Jacka, 2009). Furthermore, *suzhi* is often used to legitimize inequality by suggesting that people are responsible for their own predicaments (Murphy, 2004). Such ways of thinking about value and quality in human beings also share a resemblance with the Western version of the 'subject of value' (Skeggs, 2004; Skeggs, 2011). Skeggs's (2004) work shows how working-class women in the UK struggle to 'attach dominant symbolic value to themselves', while finding it incredibly emotionally demanding (Skeggs, 2011: 503). Ethnic performers' experiences resonate strongly with these struggles, as they also work hard to achieve valuable and respectable personhood, yet they are constrained by multi-layered social inequalities. Therefore, thinking about the self as relational is not just thinking about how individuals are embedded in social relationships and how they are shaped by social interactions with other people. It also entails considering how they are shaped by social and cultural norms revolved around gender, ethnicity, and the rural–urban divide.

Thirdly, in thinking about relationships, this approach emphasizes the impact of work and migration on personal relationships with significant others. Unlike the 'personal life' and 'intimacy' frameworks, this approach does not prioritize intimate relationships as the central focus. Rather, it regards relationships as one aspect of people's intimate negotiations. Inspired by the discussion about personal life in public space (May, 2011), this approach also considers performers' relationships, or brief encounters, with customers, and how such encounters have a deep impact on their personal lives. It further seeks to blur the line between work and non-work spheres by focusing on performers' relationships with other people, especially their significant others.

Fourthly, using intimacy as a lens, as suggested by the term itself, means regarding these intimate negotiations not just as a consequence but also as a methodological and theoretical tool to understand broader social issues. It means starting with the intimate realm and working from there to understand broader social issues. Through the lens of intimacy, I seek to explore the working mechanism of these intersecting inequalities/bordering processes, and the ways that they act upon individuals' emotions, senses of self, and relationships. Therefore, the central question that underlies this book is: what is the value of using intimacy as a lens to understand migrant performers' experiences of encountering multiple borders through work and migration? I suggest that the logical way to answer this question is through ethnography.

Researching migrant performers in Southwest China

In order to gain an understanding of how ethnic performers conduct their everyday work, and how that has an impact on their personal lives, I conducted ethnographic fieldwork in three field sites which involve ethnic performance – Waterfall Restaurant, Tea Park, and Forest Park in Green City (all pseudonyms), Southwest China. From October 2016 to April 2017, I spent a total of six months within and outside of these three sites doing participant observation and in-depth interviews with ethnic performers.

The choice of research sites and gaining access

As mentioned before, the choice of research city – Green City in Yunnan Province, Southwest China – is related to several gaps in the literature about migrant workers in China. Green City, with a population of approximately 300,000 people, becomes a good choice to explore migrants who move within provinces, in western and inland China, and to small-scale cities with more relaxed *hukou* restrictions. I decided to anonymize the name of the city since I consider it an effective way of protecting informants' identities.

With the most diverse ethnic groups in China – 25 state-recognized minority groups – Yunnan is a place known for its multi-ethnic culture, tourism, and relative lack of conflict between the different ethnic groups. That is also the reason that while minority rights in areas like Tibet and Xinjiang have attracted so much attention in the nation and worldwide, ethnic minorities in Yunnan are usually associated with harmony, exotic performance, and ethnic tourism. In 2015, in his domestic inspection tour of Yunnan, President Xi Jinping expressed his high hopes for this place, declaring that Yunnan should work hard to be a 'model region of ethnic solidarity in the nation' (People's Daily, 2015). He specifically related this prospect with the challenge of poverty elimination in Yunnan, as Yunnan is also one of the most impoverished provinces in China. In recent years, poverty elimination campaigns have proliferated in China, seeking to eliminate poverty and build a moderately prosperous society by 2020. As a result, poverty elimination and economic growth have become the major priorities for many cities and villages in Yunnan.

With 14 state-recognized ethnic groups, Green City is trying to boost its economic growth by developing local tourism, with the display of ethnic culture as a crucial element in its tourism business. A village in Green City's jurisdiction is frequently praised by both local and national media for lifting itself out of poverty by developing ethnic tourism in the village, as it has turned itself into a tourist site where tourists can come and watch ethnic performances.[1] While eager to promote ethnic tourism as part of its economic growth, multiple barriers exist for the city's ethnic performers, who are mostly rural migrants who want to settle down in the city, just like other cities in China. Tensions between desirable ethnic performance and the undesirable presence of rural migrant performers make Green City a potentially informative site for this research. The fact that I can speak the local dialect was also beneficial, enabling me to have conversations more easily with informants.

Ethnic performance indeed was burgeoning in Green City. Before I conducted the fieldwork, I only knew of two restaurants where ethnic performance was available for customers. When I undertook the fieldwork, the number had grown considerably, with an increasing number of restaurants including ethnic performance as part of their businesses. Among them, I chose one restaurant and two tourist sites to conduct the fieldwork. The next chapter provides a more detailed description of the three research sites, therefore only a brief sketch will be given here. Waterfall Restaurant is a high-end restaurant, where customers can order ethnic performance at their dining tables. The ethnic performers are waiters and waitresses in the restaurant, who dress up in ethnic costumes that are designed for on-stage performances and are ready to perform whenever required to by the customers. Tea Park and Forest Park are the two most famous tourist sites in Green City, with tea culture and animals in the forest as the major attractions for tourists. Ethnic performance shows, following a fixed schedule, are part of the routines for these two tourist sites. Additionally, tourists who choose to dine in these two locations can also ask for *bancan* (accompanying meals), which involve performers performing at their dining tables in a manner similar to Waterfall Restaurant.

Although gaining access to these field sites was easier with local networks and connections, it was not without challenges. Gaining access also involved negotiating potential roles in the field to justify my presence and also make myself useful there. After some negotiation with gatekeepers, I decided to work alongside the informants in Waterfall Restaurant as a waitress/performer, considering it is the most reasonable option for me in order to justify my presence in the semi-private settings of the individual compartments of the restaurant. In that way, I was able to observe ethnic performance without disrupting the restaurant's business. The two ethnic costumes that were designed for tourism, one representing Lahu culture and another representing Wa culture, were provided by the restaurant owner. Being dressed the same way as my informants in the restaurant and working together with them on a daily basis also became an important way for me to build rapport with them. Such options did not seem to be available in the other two places, as the bar for performers was set higher, which means more training was required. Therefore, I shadowed informants' work by being in their workplace. I also tried to make myself useful by helping to pour tea for the audiences at the performance site in Tea Park. In Forest Park, I mostly observed informants' work by being in multiple locations – backstage, offstage, and in the dining hall for *bancan*. I tried to help performers as much as I could if they needed a hand with small chores like moving costumes, sweeping the floor, and so on.

Overall, I did three months' participant observation in Waterfall Restaurant, and one month each in Tea Park and Forest Park. There was also approximately one month during which I was not at these three sites, but was mainly interviewing informants outside of them. These informants were recruited by snowball sampling using existing informants' networks.

Doing participant observation – encounters and immersion

Although I was undertaking ethnography in my own hometown, I did not consider myself to be doing research as an 'insider', since I knew little about the group of people that I was trying to learn about. The social distance between the informants and me could be large, and I initially found it difficult to have a real conversation with them. Such feelings are mutual, and some informants later told me that they initially did not know how to talk to me. For instance, Mi, after we got to know each other better, said to me: "You know, at the beginning, I really don't know what to talk to you. You are a colleague graduate with high educational level, and you always seem to work hard at the restaurant … it's a bit intimidating [to talk to you] really."

As I argue in this book, ethnic performance becomes a site of 'encounter' for performers as they experience multiple bordering processes during migration and in daily work. Similarly, for me, participant observation is not just a form of 'immersion' where the researcher seeks to 'fade into the background', but also involves encounters between the researcher and the informants, especially during the initial period of fieldwork. Such moments of encounter can be theoretically informative as well.

Shortly after I started working at Waterfall Restaurant there were rumours about me. When I was working with Mei, she said to me, "People tell me you've arrived by Mercedes the other day, is that true?" Of course it was not the case, but from that rumour I learnt how some informants imagine what 'city people' with privileges are like. Later that day, when I was sweeping the floor with Qi, who allegedly spread the rumour about me arriving in a Mercedes, she was talking about her plan to buy a good car in front of me and other workers. She said that she was saving money together with her boyfriend, hoping to buy a good-brand car pretty soon. Later I learnt that the money that they were saving was nowhere near enough to buy a car. I wonder whether Qi deliberately said such things in front of me to indicate a level of respectability (Skeggs, 1997). The initial responses from some of the informants showed their insecurity about interacting with someone from the city, and raised their fears about not being treated as respectable people – feelings that perhaps they learnt from previous interactions with urban customers and residents.

Educational level also played a role in my initial contacts with informants. Some of informants initially called me 'college girl' (*daxuesheng*). The other common thing that informants tended to say to me was that they were not sure what they possibly had to offer. Just as Woodman's (2017) informants thought that they were too little educated to have insights to help the researcher, many of my informants also shared the same sense of 'inadequacy'. They worried that their experiences were not worth telling because they were not well-educated or 'successful' from a common perspective. I generally feel that they tended to give little credit to themselves and their experiences.

Sometimes they even felt embarrassed having to share their hardships with me. Some of them kept asking in the interviews: "Am I really helping you with your research [by sharing these experiences]?" Nevertheless, I learnt a lot from the responses of informants encountering me as a researcher, and also as someone from a different socio-economic background.

Gradually, through 'immersion', as well as through showing up every day, informants got used to my presence, and got to know me as a person. Building rapport was relatively easy as we worked closely every day in Waterfall Restaurant. There were many work routines which required workers to work together in groups of two or three – sweeping the floor, clearing the tables, and waiting outside of guests' compartments in case they needed anything. These all became important moments for casual conversations between me and the informants.

Spending time together, working together, and having conversations where I tried to be as open and honest as I could about myself and my own life – these all became important ways to build rapport with informants. More importantly, by 'being there', I got a sense of what informants' mundane, everyday work lives are like. Just like many other migrant workers in China, my informants spent a lot of time at their workplace, ranging from 10 to 15 hours a day. Therefore, the workplace is a good starting point for data generation, since informants spend so much of their daily lives at work. Being at the informants' workplace also led me to recognize the important role of work in informants' personal lives. If I were not there, informants would probably just say something like "it's just work", since work is something so mundane and unremarkable. In that sense, I found participant observation useful in 'revealing the unmarked' – something so easily faded into mundane everyday lives, and not yet articulated in language or even entering the informants' consciousness (Salzinger, 2004). These reveals provide theoretical insights for researchers. By being there, and by doing some of the work myself, I demonstrated the possibility of greater empathy with informants. During interviews, some of them said things like "You were there, you know how tiring the work is", or "You know the way that some of the customers treat us".

Besides participant observation, I also conducted 60 in-depth interviews with informants within and outside of the field sites. This included 45 informants from the three field sites, and 15 informants who were recruited by snowball sampling outside the field. Of the informants, 33 were women, and 27 of them were men. Most of informants were young people aged between 16 to 30 years old (75 per cent), and most of them (64.4 per cent) were single. Most informants had an educational level of junior high school or lower (78.4 per cent). The ethnic composition of the sample included 36.7 per cent ethnic Han informants and 63.3 per cent registered as ethnic minorities, including Wa, Hani, Lahu, Yi, Dai, and Miao. Among them, most ethnic minority informants came from Wa, Lahu, or Hani backgrounds. At the same time, all informants were intra-provincial migrants from adjacent towns and villages, ranging in distance from Green City from half an hour to four hour's drive. Also, none of the informants identified themselves as belonging to the LGBT community.[2] Most of the informants fluently spoke the local dialect or Mandarin because they had been through a Han-style education system. Only three of them were not very confident in the fluency of their Mandarin or local dialect, yet I was able to comprehend what was shared with me. I am aware that those who are able to speak the local dialect in Green City may reflect an already more urbanized population; I am therefore wary of over-generalizing the findings from informants' experiences to those of ethnic minority people more generally.

In general, doing fieldwork involved many surprises, whereby my presumptions were challenged. Initially I was even a bit disappointed when I learnt that not many of the performers were 'authentic' ethnic minorities, and that they had learnt these ethnic songs and dances with a little training just like I did. Frustrated by what I found, I even questioned the value of conducting this research for a while, or wondered if I was conducting the fieldwork in the wrong place. There were other surprises as well, such as that many informants were not very keen on transferring their *hukou* to Green City, despite the fact that they were theoretically able to do so. I thought about all the literature that I had read which talked about how lacking local *hukou* is a significant impediment for migrant workers to settle in the cities, and wondered why informants did not seem to be very keen on discussing the possibility of *hukou* transfer. This '*hukou* puzzle', as Chen and Fan (2016) call it, will be explored in Chapter 3. Another surprise was that some young informants spent a lot of their hard-earned money on consumption and entertainment activities after work, such as going to night clubs and the popular 'barbecue booths'. This points to the informants' desire to switch their role from being service providers to consumers, and their anxiety to seem modern and to be recognized as someone respectable. This will be discussed in Chapter 2. These unexpected moments and surprises in the field pushed me to put aside some of my pre-existing assumptions, whether from the literature or from my imagined notions about the informants. These surprises also proved to be fruitful later in the analysis process when I started writing the research findings about the informants, and tried to understand them through a sociological lens. They went on to become prominent themes in this book.

Outline of the book

The next chapter provides a detailed description of ethnic performers' work, theorizes the meaning of ethnic performance, and uses it as the starting point of this inquiry. I show how ethnic performance is a form of interactive service work, as it involves physically close interactions between guests and performers. Different theoretical frameworks are explored in relation to understanding the meaning of ethnic performance. Such exploration shows how a single framework cannot capture the complexity and multiple dimensions of ethnic performance work. Therefore, borrowing the idea of 'service encounters' (Hanser, 2008), I argue that ethnic performance could best be theorized as a 'site of encounter', where people from different social positions interact with each other in a close manner. Here, 'encounter' has another level of meaning, as it also refers to how migrant performers have to constantly encounter bordering processes, most notably revolving around rural–urban migration, ethnicity, and gender. I discuss the ways borders proliferate in performers' everyday work and migration journeys as a result of the intersection between capital, mobility, and labour regimes (Mezzadra and Neilson, 2013). Two cases regarding performers' sense of entitlement to respect and also their off-work entertainment are used to discuss why the border encounters are always intimate, emotional, and personal, illustrating why the lens of intimacy should be used to understand these encounters.

Chapter 3 discusses how, as rural–urban migrants, the most significant border they have to encounter is the *hukou* system, which makes their performances, but not their presence in the city, desirable. It explores how migrants use their emotional reflexivity to make sense of an opaque migration regime and how this emotional reflexivity is heavily informed by the current emotional regime which promotes personal responsibilities. The different cultural meanings assigned to the rural and the urban also play a role in shaping performers' senses of self and emotions. The lens of intimacy allows us to see how the border crossing of the rural and the urban is fundamentally emotional.

Chapter 4 explores how working as ethnic performers means that informants have to encounter ethnicity in their everyday work and are subject to 'ethnic assessment' according to pre-existing social scripts about ethnicity in China. I call these cultural normative assumptions about ethnicity 'ethnic scripts', and explore how performers' ambivalences toward their ethnic identities enables us to think about ethnicity as something we do, rather than as something we are. I also explore how the commercialization of ethnicity pushes informants to work on their emotions and senses of self in a way that accords with ethnic scripts in China. Here, the lens of intimacy leads us to rethink the meaning of being ethnic in contemporary China in an innovative way.

In Chapter 5, I explore how the lens of intimacy also illuminates how performers' work and lives are governed by the gendered aspects of bordering. I discuss the different ways that female performers and male performers negotiate undertaking sexualized labour in ethnic performances, and how gender is negotiated in close association with ethnic scripts. The ways that undertaking sexualized labour overshadows female performers' intimate relationships with significant others also reveals how work increasingly overtakes our 'private' lives. Focusing on these intimate negotiations is crucial in revealing the working mechanisms of borders and how they proliferate in performers' migration journeys, as well as everyday work.

This book concludes in Chapter 6 by further discussing the potential of intimacy as a lens in revealing the social, and how it can be an important part of an intimate turn to understand 'the cultural politics of inequality' (Sun, 2013, 2023).

2

Ethnic Performance Work

This chapter provides a detailed account of what ethnic performance is like at these three field sites: Waterfall Restaurant, Tea Park, and Forest Park. It demonstrates how ethnic performance is fundamentally a form of interactive service work, as *bancan* (accompanying meals) is the most important part of a performer's work. Performers' affective labour helps guests' *guanxi*-building (relationship-building) processes as they turn cold, calculated relationships into ones rooted in sentiment and affect. In this sense, migrant performers constantly struggle with their desirable performances and undesirable presence in the city (as migrants without local *hukou*). This chapter engages with different sociological concepts and theories, such as 'the cultural authority of the state' (Nyiri, 2010), 'affective labour' (Hardt, 1999), and 'gender as a frame' (Ridgeway, 2009, 2011), to theorize the meaning of ethnic performance. While these concepts illuminate different aspects of ethnic performance, this chapter further demonstrates how ethnic performance could be best theorized as a site of encounter. This, on the one hand, means that the service encounter between performers and customers, due to the nature of interactive service work, requires that they interact with each other in a physically proximate manner. On the other hand, ethnic performance is also a site where performers have to constantly encounter multiple bordering processes related to the rural–urban divide, ethnicity, and gender. Such encounters are intimate, personal, and emotional – as shown through the examples of performers' senses of entitlement to respect and their consumption and entertainment activities. These intimate border encounters also point to the need to see work and personal life as closely related and mutually constitutive, rather than different spheres with clear boundaries. This chapter lays a foundation for later chapters in theorizing the usefulness of the lens of intimacy to understand these border struggles and experiences of border encounters of migrant performers.

Working as an ethnic performer

This section provides a detailed description of how performance work was organized and conducted in the three field sites, which offers readers a glimpse of what is like to work as an ethnic performer at the frontier of service work.

Waterfall Restaurant is a high-end *nongjiale* (rural tourism) restaurant in Green City. *Nongjiale* restaurants have gained popularity among Chinese urban dwellers over the past 10 years. Aiming to provide authentic, rustic food from the countryside, *nongjiale* restaurants are embodiments of how romanticized rurality becomes a nostalgic ideal for urbanites (Park, 2014). Indeed, Waterfall Restaurant's building and environment seek to make guests feel that they have entered a rural villager's house. Upon entering the restaurant, what first appears is a courtyard, which resembles that of a farmer's house. There are some vegetables and plants growing in a small plot, with corn cobs hanging on the pillars to create a harvest scene. On a sunny day in October 2016, when I first walked into the restaurant, I saw waiters and waitresses dressed in colourful minority clothes having a rest in the yard. It does appear to be an impressive scene for outside visitors. In the restaurant, the main dining area is a three-floored building with ten compartments designed for guests – each small room only accommodates one table of customers, which allows guests privacy during their meal. In the carefully decorated compartments, there are pictures and drawings of ethnic minority women hanging on the wall, which again suggests this is a high-end *nongjiale* restaurant with local ethnic characteristics. All these suggest that this is not a cheap place to have a meal, which is also reflected in the price: a table of food for around ten people cost between 600 yuan to 1,000 yuan in 2016, while a performer's monthly wage stood at 2,000 yuan.

In Waterfall Restaurant, ethnic performances are undertaken by waiters and waitresses working in the restaurant. Their working uniforms are minority costumes provided by the restaurant owner – two sets of minority clothes (Wa and Lahu), which are both colourful and distinctive from Han costumes. Working in Waterfall Restaurant is demanding and tiring. The working hours are long – usually from 8 am until 10 pm. Sometimes it can even stretch later into the night, depending on how late the guests stay. In such a popular restaurant with guests constantly coming and going, workers not only have to wait tables and constantly respond to guests' need, they also have to constantly switch their roles to performers since they need to perform songs and toasting rituals whenever such performances are required by the guests. Ethnic performance is considered as an integral part of waiters' and waitresses' work, and therefore is not remunerated separately.

A typical night at Waterfall Restaurant unfolds as guests arrive for dinner at around 6 pm. By that time, workers in the restaurant would have worked for seven hours, since their workday starts at 8 am with only a short break in the middle. They take shifts in doing tasks such as cleaning, buying vegetables from the market, serving guests who come for lunch, and doing preparation work for guests who come in for dinner – such as setting the tables, cleaning the compartments, and getting pre-ordered menus ready. They normally have a quick dinner at 4 pm each day before the guests arrive (see Figure 2.1). Dinner time is often the busiest time of the day, since they have to find time to perform for guests among their already demanding service work.

Ethnic performance can be requested for free by dining guests at Waterfall Restaurant. When it is called upon, everyone has to put aside their current service work and appear in front of the customers. Performances do not just entail singing minority songs in front of guests. While singing, performers have to take it in turns to massage guests' shoulders while proposing toasts to them with strong alcoholic liquor – usually not in a negotiable way since competitive drinking is also an essential ritual during Chinese banquets (Kipnis, 1997; Mason, 2013). 'You can't stop drinking while the song is still going on' (*geshengbuting jiubuting*) was a phrase often used by performers to justify the compulsory drinking ritual. Sometimes they also justify it by

Figure 2.1: Performers at Waterfall Restaurant having an early dinner at 4 pm, so that they will be ready to serve dining guests throughout the night. Photo taken by author.

stating that it is part of the minority's culture. Every guest takes turns to enjoy this service – listening to songs while being massaged by an opposite-sex performer, as well as being the target of compulsory drinking. The atmosphere at the performance is often lively and passionate, with guests laughing, watching, and taking photos of the unique scene. The performance only ends when the guests say that performers can leave, at which point performers will switch their roles back to being waiters and waitresses. Their workload will increase at that point, since there will be unanswered calls from other customers.

Working as both waiters and performers in Waterfall Restaurant is certainly not an easy job. Performers have to shift between two different roles very quickly, and the work is generally tiring and demanding. One might ask who these performers are. Are they professionally trained to be performers? Furthermore, while dressing up as ethnic minorities and performing minority songs, do these performances have anything to do with performers' ethnic identities? I will come back to these questions after describing the kind of performances at two tourist sites in Green City – Tea Park and Forest Park.

Ethnic performance has become an important tourist attraction for visitors in Tea Park, alongside other attractions such as the Tea Museum, tea plantations, and temples to worship tea ancestors. The ethnic performance was initially designed to showcase that tea is an integral part of many minorities' everyday lives and is rooted in their cultures. There is one room named Lahu People's Home (*lahuzhijia*) in the Tea Park. It is a medium-sized room with performances taking place there three times a day following a fixed schedule. Performances here are more stage-oriented, with performers being trained and the shows rehearsed. Without a clearly identified stage, the audience sits quite close to performers to watch their performances while drinking the tea (brewed using minority brewing methods) offered to them by the performers. With the fireplace burning, the tea brewing, and the minority performance going on, such minority song and dance shows seek to make the guests feel that they are actually enjoying tea in a minority family's kitchen.

The content of the show usually includes five to six songs and dances from different ethnicities, usually featuring the minority cultures of Wa, Lahu, Dai, and Hani, which are the major minority groups that live around Green City. They are all undertaken by the same group of performers, which means that performers have to change costumes during the gaps between performances in order to dress up as minorities from different groups. The performance lasts around half an hour, usually with an opening song to welcome the guests' arrival, and a farewell song dedicated to them leaving.

Aside from the on-stage performance, another major part of a performer's work is to *bancan*, which literally means 'accompanying meals'. This type of work largely resembles what performers are doing in Waterfall Restaurant.

That is, they are performing minority songs to boost the atmosphere at the banquet table. They are also doing a series of tasks including urging guests to compulsory drink, proposing toasts, and sometimes having bodily contact with guests as well, such as massaging guests' shoulders, drinking cross-cupped wine[1] with guests, and so on.

The same activities of *bancan* also manifest themselves in Forest Park, although with a higher frequency – workers have to perform these tasks on a daily basis apart from their routine work of on-stage performance. This is because Forest Park is much larger in scale, with groups of tourists coming to visit every day. In fact, Forest Park is the biggest attraction in the local area. It is a national park with an ancient forest and different kinds of animals. It usually takes two to three hours to have a tour in the park, during which time ethnic performance is one of the attractions available for visitors to watch. The performance is formal in status compared to those at the other two sites. It resembles a professional show in a theatre with well-rehearsed minority songs and dances, as well as well-trained, semi-professional performers. The lighting effects, sound effects, and carefully decorated stage all point to the professionalism of the show. The show lasts for about half an hour, with the same group of performers dressed as different ethnic minority groups and performing diverse minority songs and dances.

Tourists who have dinner in Forest Park have the chance to enjoy performers' *bancan* at the dinner table while they are having meals (see Figure 2.2). In a

Figure 2.2: *Bancan* at Forest Park. Photo taken by author.

way, the Forest Park *bancan* partly resembles that in Waterfall Restaurant, with performances of songs and dances used to boost atmosphere at the dinner tables and the proposing of toasts and competitive drinking being important rituals. On the other hand, *bancan* here is more organized and professional, with a host organizing the whole process. There are also more activities involved in *bancan* in Forest Park. For example, performers are normally expected to have cross-cupped wine with customers, usually with the opposite sex. Hosts will usually present the performances in a stand-up comedy style, with jokes and stories that are supposed to introduce minority cultures and traditions to the guests. For VIP clients – managers' friends, superiors, and local cadres – more exotic 'minority rituals' are provided, which include female performers sitting on male customers' laps while other performers force wine down the guests' throats. With the *bancan*, guests' dining tables are always filled with laughter, songs, and cameras to record the special scenes. I also heard some tourists, especially those who came from outside of Yunnan Province, comment that they felt like they had only actually experienced the local ethnic flavours after the *bancan*.

In summary, there are different dynamics in working as ethnic performers in these three sites. What is common among them is the fact that performers' work not only includes the performance of songs and dances, but also comprises various service tasks – waitressing, toasting, entertaining guests, and so on. In the next section, I will engage with different sociological concepts and theories to further explore the multi-layered meaning of ethnic performance, highlighting it as an important site to understand the intertwining inequalities of the rural–urban divide, ethnicity, and gender in China.

Exploring the multi-layered meaning of ethnic performance
Performing ethnicity under the cultural authority of the state

First and foremost, ethnic performance involves what I call 'performing ethnicity', which means that performers' exoticized bodies and presences are used to convey a sense of multi-ethnic culture, which in turn is promoted in nation-state rhetoric and embraced by the market economy. Ethnic performance was worth viewing from tourists' perspective exactly because it is something extraordinary – something alien from most tourists' everyday lives. It is under such circumstances that the performances can attract 'the tourist gaze' (Urry, 2002). This attraction is also based on tourists' craving to view 'authentic' ethnic culture as part of living in the modern era (MacCannell, 1973); such craving further serves to reaffirm tourists' position as modern Han citizens (Walsh and Swain, 2004). Therefore, it is

Figure 2.3: Ethnic performers under the 'Han gaze'. Photo taken by author.

also a form of 'Han gaze' which puts minority people in the position of the objects that are being viewed, while Han audiences are the viewers under whose gaze ethnic minority people are exoticized and eroticized (Schein, 2000) (see Figure 2.3).

Both the tourists' gaze and the Han gaze are carefully guided and shaped by 'the cultural authority of the state' (Nyíri, 2006; Nyíri, 2010). The cultural authority of the state in tourism shows through its framing of the meaning of such scenic spots. It advances a set of clear and hegemonic narratives about how tourists should interpret the meanings of scenic spots (Nyíri, 2006). For example, billboards and signs are certainly one mechanism that the state is using to affirm its 'cultural authority' over scenic points. Once one steps out of the airport of Green City, one can see billboards and signs erected by the local tourist bureau inviting one to 'Search for the most authentic ethnic cultures in Green City', or 'Be ready to meet with the most sincere and passionate greetings from minority people'. Ethnic minority culture is promoted alongside Green City's fresh air and lush forests as the attractions of Green City's tourism business. In this way, the state directs the tourists' gaze and influences how tourists are expected to view things that they encounter in the tourism journey. Certain scenic spots in China are also curated and mobilized to educate tourists as patriotic citizens (Nyíri, 2006; Rippa, 2020). As mentioned before, Yunnan is a place that is known for its multi-ethnic culture and its relative lack of ethnic conflict, and was expected to become 'a model region of ethnic solidarity for the nation'. The development of ethnic tourism in Green City was certainly also shaped by such an ideology to showcase its colourful ethnic cultures and further engender tourists' nationalist pride.

The ways in which ethnic performances are designed and framed, therefore, reaffirm the cultural authority of the state. In Forest Park, before each performance starts, a host introduces the show to the general audience by providing a brief introduction of the relevant minority culture and its traditions. This introduction is largely similar to the textbook introduction of ethnic minorities in China. It resembles the official discourses of ethnic minorities – such as how they are born to be naturally good at singing and dancing and how they used to live in primitive ways but were saved by the socialist regime. Such introductions, in accordance with the scripted shows that follow, reinforce official views and portray stereotypes of ethnic minority people in China (see, for example, Gladney, 1994; Harrell, 1995). Once, I heard a member of an audience expressing his opinions about the show: "I have never encountered a real ethnic minority person in my life before. The show is magnificent! I feel that I have seen what I have read from textbooks about minority people for the first time in real life." This audience member's reflection reveals how ethnic minorities are under-represented in many parts of China, and invisible in most people's ordinary and mundane lives. It is in that context that the tourist gaze is successfully constituted, as it falls upon something that departs from the tourists' ordinary, mundane routines (Urry, 2002). When they do appear, representations of ethnic minority people tend to be shown in a strictly scripted and managed way.

However, interestingly, the people who are 'performing ethnicity' are not necessarily ethnic minorities themselves. Some of the performers are Han Chinese, and some of them are officially registered as ethnic minorities but do not think of themselves as authentic minority people. In fact, less than half of the performers in the three sites identify themselves as genuine ethnic minorities. There is also a general trend in all these sites that Han people are increasingly taking over ethnic performance work, since they are deemed by the managers to be more professional and manageable compared to minority people. Senior workers in Waterfall Restaurant told me of an incident when a group of Wa performers had decided to strike a few years ago, and had walked out of their jobs on that same day, resulting in the closure of the restaurant for several days. After that, the restaurant manager decided to no longer hire a lot of performers from the same ethnic background since they, according to the manager, "share too much solidary" (*tai tuanjie le*), and are therefore "difficult to manage" (*bu hao guan*). It is telling how, instead of improving working conditions, the manager decided to hire more Han people to solve the problem of workers striking based on a shared ethnicity. It is also revealing that ethnic minorities are further marginalized and excluded from jobs that seem to be specifically designed for them.

From the management perspective, singing minority songs does not require much professional skill or knowledge of ethnic cultures, and therefore it can be easily learned. Han performers themselves understand little of the meanings of the songs that they are performing, and they usually memorize the lyrics with the aid of *pinyin* – the romanized spelling of Mandarin. Therefore, it is worth exploring whether the work of ethnic performers would necessarily have something to do with one's ethnic identity, and if so, in what ways. I will discuss such dynamics in more detail in Chapter 4, where I explore questions of ethnicity. But it is important to point out here the tension that a performer's work involves: they must perform as an 'authentic ethnic minority' person to meet the expectation of the tourist's gaze despite their ambivalent feelings about their ethnic identity. Concepts such as 'tourist gaze' and 'Han gaze' cannot fully capture how people experience such work from their own point of view. Also, performers' work does not only involve being gazed at from a distance, but also includes frequent in-person interactions with guests. It is with these considerations in mind that I turn to theorizing the other dimension of ethnic performance – service work.

Doing affective labour at the banqueting tables

Ethnic performance is fundamentally a form of service work, as *bancan* at the guests' banqueting tables is in fact the most important part of the performers' work. Since *bancan* involves physical proximity, and sometimes even intimate interactions between performers and guests as previously noted, it is a form of 'interactive service work' (Leidner, 1991). Such work brings the production and consumption of service into the same time and space, with the quality of such work largely determined by the interaction between service providers and guests (Urry, 2002).

Therefore, ethnic performance embodies drastically different dynamics compared to factory work, which is the major focus of previous literature on rural–urban labour migration in China. Unlike factory work, which arguably mainly involves workers working alone facing a machine most of the time, service work involves close interactions between service providers and receivers. Such physical proximity brings new challenges to migrants which are lived through their intimate lives, and have an impact on their emotions, sense of self, and intimate relationships with others, as this book seeks to demonstrate.

For example, ethnic performers, who are also waiters and waitresses, inevitably need to undertake 'emotional labour' to regulate their own emotions in the service process (Hochschild, 1983) to ensure that it is a pleasurable experience for the guests. They are also, implicitly or explicitly, required to do a substantial amount of 'aesthetic labour', regulating their physical appearances to be aesthetically pleasing and attractive (Witz et al, 2003; Warhurst and Nickson, 2009). In fact, their youth and aesthetically pleasing appearance are a requisite for them to be hired in the first place. There are also constant reminders during work that they should work hard to keep appearing attractive. Sometimes managers directly comment upon someone's *yanzhi* in the presence of other workers. *Yanzhi*, a popularized word from the internet, literally means that a person's degree of good looks can be calculated into a numerical value. By measuring performers by their *yanzhi*, especially female performers, the pressure of doing aesthetic labour is internalized by many workers as a legitimate part of the work. In the context of ethnic performance, aesthetic labour may have another layer of meaning, since the expectation is that performers should look like authentic ethnic minorities. Their bodies become the sites where different aesthetic standards and different expectations of what constitutes an authentic minority are projected, since guests are expected to encounter the imagined otherness of ethnic minorities through the embodied work of ethnic performers (see also Grillot and Zhang, 2016). At the same time, performers' work is also highly gendered and sexualized in many ways. The most notorious example is how female performers are sometimes expected to sit on the laps of male guests while toasting. Sometimes sexual harassment from guests is even legitimated as part of the work. I will theorize the impact upon performers undertaking sexualized work in more detail in Chapter 5.

Another way to consider the different aspects of labour that ethnic performers are expected to do is to employ the concept of 'affective labour'. Unlike emotional labour, which is more about how people manage their own emotions inwardly (Hochschild, 1983), affective labour points to the dimensions of labour which are closely associated with 'the creation and manipulation of affects' (Hardt, 1999: 96). Performers are not just managing their own emotions, but also creating a 'vibe' or 'atmosphere' which contributes to the guests' banqueting. They do so by using various types of bodily work and emotional work, which involves not only singing and dancing, but also serving guests in a physically close manner – even having bodily contact with them, as described before. Through this work, they are trying to engender and manage certain affects at the banqueting table, such as excitement, pleasure, sense of intimacy, and even a sense of nationalist pride. To better understand what performers are expected to achieve by undertaking affective labour, it is necessary to first gain an understanding of the social and cultural meaning of banqueting in China in general.

Bancan should be understood in relation to China's banqueting and business entertainment customs. Banqueting and competitive drinking have long been recognized as an important way for people to build up *guanxi* (relationships, networks, or connections) in China (Kipnis, 1997).

Since the rise of marketization in the 1980s, banqueting has become an important way for government officials and business elites to build up and maintain *guanxi* (see, for example, Osburg, 2013). For them, banqueting and drinking has even become an integral part of their job outside of office hours and spaces, since it is an effective way to get things done (Mason, 2013). The important roles of emotions and feelings in *guanxi*-building has been increasingly highlighted by scholars (Barbalet, 2018), and successful banquet and business entertainment should be able to turn 'interested, calculated, commodified relationships into ones rooted in "irrational" sentiment and affect' (Osburg, 2013: 33). Doing so requires having shared experiences of pleasure and intimacy during business entertainment, which was previously usually achieved by going to places such as karaoke bars, massage parlours, and so on. Sex services are sometimes included, as being able to do illicit things together shows a certain level of trust (Osburg, 2013).

However, things have changed at the official level since Osburg's fieldwork was undertaken from 2002 to 2006. In 2012, President Xi launched an austerity campaign against extravagant consumption and corruption by officials. The sites that used to be important for elite entertainment became no longer acceptable – at least on paper. Government officials and public servants were even formally banned from entering karaoke clubs. This major change means that banqueting and business entertaining need to be conducted in a much more legitimate and discreet form. Sites where ethnic performance is conducted seem like a safe choice, since promoting local ethnic culture and celebrating the multi-ethnic culture of the state seem politically expedient. Dining in Waterfall Restaurant, which claims to be a *nongjiale* restaurant, might seem to avoid the appearance of extravagant spending, although the price of banqueting there suggests a different story.

It is in these contexts that the meaning of ethnic performance as a form of affective labour should be reconsidered in relation to the changing landscape of business entertainment, as well as the generally unchanging banqueting culture in China. I argue that the things that performers are doing during *bancan* – through singing, urging guests to drink, proposing toasts, and sometimes even having bodily contact with guests – are all important ways to create certain atmospheres and sentiments at guests' banqueting tables, thereby also contributing to guests' *guanxi*-building processes (see also Mao, 2021). This is not to deny the existence of emotional labour in ethnic performance. In fact, certain affects are only successfully conveyed due to the performers undertaking emotional labour to manage their own emotions, as well as the body work which involves aesthetic labour and sexualized labour.

Despite the fact that the concept of 'affective labour' can enhance our understanding of how performers' labour is used to contribute to guests' *guanxi*-building processes, it cannot capture the complexity, nor the multidimensionality, of ethnic performance as a form of labour. It also cannot capture the multiple tensions that inherently lie within performers' labour. One such tension is how performers' labour is a desired, while their presence in the cities is not. In an ethnographical study about ethnic Yao people who travel across the Sino-Vietnam border to occasionally perform ethnic songs and dances in China (and who lack any official identity in China, rendering them 'illegal' migrants), Barabantseva (2015) convincingly argues that they are desirable and disposable at the same time. While their performances are desirable to showcase China's multi-ethnic culture, their presence is not, since they are illegal migrants without legitimate visas (Barabantseva, 2015). In a similar vein, migrant performers also face the tension of their performances being desired, on the one hand, and their presence as migrants without *hukou* being undesired on the other. In contrast to the migration of Yao people, this 'differential inclusion' (Mezzadra and Neilson, 2013) happens within the national border, but their relationships with the local population in the area to which they migrate is nonetheless analogous. Another tension lies in how performers' affective labour is used to facilitate intimacy, which is a crucial component of China's capitalist economic mode (Osburg, 2013), while their own time and space for intimacy is compromised under the exploitative labour regime which squeezes the already limited time they have for families and friends – a point I will demonstrate in the following section. In a chapter titled 'Love and gold', A.R. Hochschild provides a powerful metaphor which effectively captures how a nanny's love and care – like gold – are extracted from the Global South, and re-implanted to middle-class families in the Global North (Hochschild, 2003). Such a metaphor could also be employed to theorize the a performer's dilemma of undertaking affective labour while compromising their own intimate space.

While 'affective labour' cannot capture the multidimensional meaning of performers' labour, it also cannot capture the power relations that are at play in shaping the service encounters. It is evident – as I will show in the next section – that the different social positions of performers and guests profoundly shaped how the service work was undertaken. To be more specific, the power disparity between rural, ethnic, and often feminized service providers and the urban, Han, masculine consumers largely shaped the process of service work, which had implications for the ethnic performers. Therefore, with important insights gained from concepts such as 'the cultural authority of the state' and 'affective labour', I argue that ethnic performance could be better theorized as a site of encounters.

Ethnic performance as a site of encounters

Considering ethnic performance as a site of encounters firstly points to the need to consider the social forces that are shaping such encounters, for example, ethnicity, gender, and the rural–urban divide. It also means considering ethnic performance as a site where different forms of mobility come together – the tourists' mobility and the migrant workers' mobility. The different forms of mobility are all under the cultural authority of the state, and are ascribed with different values. The mobility regime also shapes the organization of labour, and therefore shapes the production of capital. Inspired by the work of Mezzadra and Neilson (2013), I will also consider ethnic performance as a site where different forms of borders were produced and maintained, and where border struggles proliferated.

The idea of theorizing service work as a form of encounter is inspired by Amy Hanser's (2008) work about service encounters in the context of retail business in urban China. Hanser (2008) proposes the concept of 'distinction work' to compellingly show how social distinction was produced at both organizational and interactional levels. One of the ways that such 'distinction work' is fulfilled is through the interactions between service workers and customers, during which workers need to act in a way that recognizes customers' status as respectable urban consumers with economic power and cultural tastes. Gender also plays a crucial role in the construction of 'distinction work', as organizations heavily rely on workers' gendered and sexualized bodies to send messages about distinctions and class (Hanser, 2005). Hence, numerous 'service encounters' reveal how symbolic boundaries are transformed into social boundaries, and what inequality feels like to people (Hanser, 2008).

Building on this work, I aim to further develop the idea of 'encounter' in the context of ethnic performance work, and use it to refer not only to the physical interaction between workers and guests, but also to the ways that workers experience various bordering processes through work and migration. I will also highlight performers' own emotional and intimate experiences of such encounters, hence illustrating the value of intimacy as a lens in understanding their experiences of border encounters. Furthermore, it is crucial to think about the broader social and cultural context that shapes such encounters. While Hanser's work lies in a context in which 'class' is the most prominent feature that shapes the service encounter in ethnic performance, ethnicity is the most crucial element (though this does not mean that class and ethnicity are not mutually shaped and intertwined in China's context).

Encountering ethnicity, gender and the rural–urban divide

Most notably, ethnic performance as a site of encounters is 'framed by ethnicity', in the same sense that social interactions are 'framed by gender' (Ridgeway, 2009). By 'gender as a frame', Ridgeway means the ways that gender works as a primary frame whenever and wherever we step into a social situation in order to relate with other people. For example, we need to use our common knowledge about gender to situate a person as male or female before we can engage in any form of social interaction with him or her, with a failure to do so resulting in undesirable consequences (Ridgeway, 2009, 2011). At the same time, although gender exists as the primary frame, it also constantly intersects with other institutionalized rules and cultural norms. In the case of ethnic performance, ethnicity also becomes an important frame that deeply shapes social interaction between guests and performers, since most guests are led to believe, and are constantly reminded, that they are interacting with 'authentic' ethnic minority people.

Performers' work uniforms – minority costumes with bright colours and sparkling decorations – loudly broadcast their differences. These are not the costumes minority people would usually wear in their everyday lives, but are designed for on-stage shows. With their unique looks, such clothes clearly set them apart from other people in the restaurant. Wearing stylized ethnic costumes is a crucial part of the visual representation of ethnic 'Others' that meets the expectations of guests while also conforming to the popular conceptualization of what ethnic minority people should look like according to mainstream media and state discourse; it also carries 'certain shared, social understandings and meanings about the nation and its people' (Chio, 2014: 157). I myself wore these clothes when I was working at Waterfall Restaurant. I noticed how different I felt the moment I put on the minority costume. On my walk from home to the restaurant, people were constantly staring at me. In the workplace, guests often took out phones to take pictures of me with other performers. Some of them would also ask me where I was from, and what kind of *minzu* I belonged to. I felt that I had become an object of their gaze the moment that I changed into my costume. It is therefore not surprising that performers would quickly change their costumes immediately after finishing work, even if it was only a short walk from the restaurant to their dormitories.

Indeed, the minority clothes that performers wear constantly mark the distinction between Han audiences and the performers. I remember sitting on the stairs with other performers in these clothes while some male customers passed by staring at us. One of them looked down and asked us, "Aren't you cold in these clothes?" Without waiting for our response, another man said, "That's how minority people are. They are not afraid of coldness, and they sit on the ground all the time." At that time, none of us said anything. I found such responses ironic because none of us sitting there were 'authentic' minority people – a concept that I will look at more critically in Chapter 4. Yet our dresses and body images seemed to further strengthen the stereotypes of ethnic minority people. Such small encounters are common in performers' work, during which time they are constantly exposed to audiences' comments and questions about their ethnic identities. Those performers who do not identify themselves as belonging to an ethnic minority often make up something when being asked questions by the guests. It is an unspoken rule that the audiences must be given the impression that they are meeting 'authentic' ethnic minorities. At the same time, the environment and the settings of the sites where ethnic performance takes place also constantly remind guests that they are interacting with ethnic minority people. This, as I show, has inevitably shaped the interaction between performers and guests.

At the same time, the service encounters are also 'framed by gender' (Ridgeway, 2009), and the gendered frame intersects with the ethnic frame in various ways. As mentioned before, the content of the ethnic performance and *bancan* mostly reproduce 'the Han gaze' (Schein, 2000), which shows the image of ethnic minority people in Southwest China as being exotic and erotic. Under this Han gaze, ethnic minority men and women are both feminized.

For example, the songs that are performed are the popularized versions of minority songs, which usually romanticize minority peoples' intimate relationships, with strong sexual connotations. There is one song that is especially popular which is titled 'If you are going to visit me tonight'. It tells a story of a young beautiful minority woman waiting for her lover to come to visit her. It ends with her singing, 'If you want to visit me tonight, visit me during my dream, then you can do whatever you want to do with me'. It shows the stereotype of minority women as more open and sexually available (Gladney, 1994; Schein, 2000). Guests would laugh every time they heard this song, especially male guests, some of whom would keep repeating the lyrics and telling dirty jokes after the song ended. In addition, the introductory lines from the host during *bancan* at Forest Park also bore a strong sense of gendered and sexualized bias and prejudice. In order to achieve the 'fun' atmosphere, the host would tell jokes intimating that minority people are born with passionate hearts and fall in love quickly with other people. Such ways of framing the service encounter also shaped how performers and guests interacted with each other.

It is also notable that the customers who require the most extensive service are normally urban elite men, as *guanxi*-building through banqueting is a male-dominated activity. As mentioned before, sometimes female performers are required to sit on the laps of male customers while toasting. In a way, female performers are 'projecting the idealized masculinity' to the male customers (Osburg, 2013: 10) – as both female workers and as ethnic minority women who are often imagined to be more sexually open (see, for example, Walsh, 2005). These all point to the sexualized and gendered nature of ethnic performance. However, it poses different challenges for male and female performers when undertaking such work. Their intimate negotiations regarding gender at the frontier of ethnic performance will be explored further in Chapter 5.

In a similar vein, ethnic performance as a site of encounters is also shaped by other important social divisions – most notably the rural–urban divide. As shown before, the performance sites are embodiments of how the countryside is romanticized in rural tourism. The correlation between ethnic minority people and the rustic aspects of country people is deliberately enhanced. The accents and bodily features of performers are also used as markers to draw distinctions between the rural and the urban. I will further discuss what it is like having to encounter the rural–urban divide during the everyday working life of performers in Chapter 3.

In summary, the ways that performers encounter guests during work, and the ways they encounter the bordering process which ascribes different meanings to the rural and the urban, masculinity and femininity, and the ethnic minority and Han, speak volumes about the existence of multiple borders shaping their lives. Thus, in a sense, encountering and experiencing borders have become parts of the performers' everyday lives. This often leads to fierce 'border struggles', that is, the constant negotiation around 'the ever more unstable line between the "inside" and the "outside", between inclusion and exclusion' (Mezzadra and Neilson, 2013: 13). Meanwhile, even within the national geographical borders, there are different migration and labour regimes that differentiate and make distinctions between people. Therefore, it is also important to consider the labour and mobility consequences of these bordering practices, and how they constantly rely on the aforementioned divisions of rural–urban, ethnicity, and gender to enable the expansion of the frontier of capital.

Bordering processes – mobility, labour, and the expansion of the frontier of capital

The commodification of ethnicity is economically significant, as ethnic tourism plays an increasingly important role in the local economy. The development of tourism in Green City 'stems from nothing, and grows into prosperity',[2] and from 2006 to 2015 the city's revenue tripled. The flourishing ethnic tourism in Green City was clearly evident to me. During my fieldwork from 2016 to 2017 in Green City, several new restaurants and bars opened that employed ethnic performance to attract guests. There was also a Lahu village in a town adjacent to Green City that had turned itself from an ordinary village into an ethnic theme park that included ethnic performance and charged visitors entrance fees. The village has been widely promoted in the local and national media, as it has successfully achieved poverty alleviation through the revenues earned from ethnic tourism. This has shown how the cultural authority of the state in regulating scenic points does not just lie in its framing of the meanings of the tourist scene (Nyíri, 2006). The state is also a 'curator' of ethnic differences, as it plays an active role in staging ethnic culture to boost the economy of underdeveloped areas. Such curation means that the state does not erase traditional cultures altogether, but selects and takes out the desirable parts, makes them hyper-visible, and then presents them as traditional cultures (Rippa, 2020). This is certainly true in the case of Green City, which is located in one of the most impoverished provinces in China. With a strong imperative to boost the local economy through (ethnic) tourism, both state and market actors actively mobilize the bordering between ethnic minorities and the Han in order to make profits and to also achieve a political agenda. However, a contradiction arises when ethnic performance becomes increasingly important in a local economy, as performers overwhelmingly work in exploitative labour conditions, and their mobility and settlement continue to be problematized because of the lack of local *hukou*.

Borders do not just divide, they also connect. In *Border as Methods*, Mezzadra and Neilson (2013) use the examples of financial traders and care workers to show how these two seemingly different groups are actually intimately linked – the high mobility of financial traders is enabled by the affective labour of the care workers, even though the two groups enjoy very different degrees of financial reward and their mobility is constrained in drastically different ways. In a similar vein, ethnic performance could be understood as a site in which different forms of mobility come together and are inscribed with different cultural values. For tourists, who are mostly urban middle-class people, tourism becomes a way to consume culture and improve cultural taste. It is also an important way for them to exercise their class privilege. In that sense, tourists' mobility is desirable and is in fact promoted by the state. At the same time, the mobility of performers, who are mostly rural migrants, is encouraged and facilitated because their labour is desired in the city. However, their settlement and entitlement are problematized by means of *hukou*. Here, *hukou* works as a bordering device which ensures the 'differential inclusion' of migrants (Mezzadra and Neilson, 2013; Johnson, 2017), and structures their entitlement and settlement in the city.

Moreover, the differential inclusion of migrants, together with the mobility regime, also intersects with labour regimes in various ways for migrant performers. Rural migrants disproportionally feature in informal, precarious, and flexible employment compared to their urban counterparts. Capitalist employers actively mobilize the bordering between rural and urban, as they manage to substantially lower labour cost by employing an informal and precarious labour force, which is made up of mostly rural–urban migrants (Zhang, 2021). Therefore, like migrant workers in factories who mostly work under precarious conditions and for prolonged hours (see Pun, 2005; Chan et al, 2013; Chan, 2014), migrant performers in service work settings also work under exploitative labour conditions, though these conditions tend to be less theorized than factory work. The working conditions of migrant performers are apparent most obviously through workplace rules.

As mentioned before, most migrant performers work for long hours, ranging from 10 hours to 15 hours a day. While in Waterfall Restaurant, *bancan* is an integral part of waiters and waitresses' work; in the other two sites, *bancan* is extra labour for which performers receive separate remuneration (each performer will normally earn 30 yuan extra for each *bancan* that they participate in). While *bancan* offers a channel for performers to supplement their meagre basic wage, it also means that they need to overwhelmingly undertake overtime work. Like many other rural–urban migrants in the informal service sector, one common characteristic of such work environments is that they tend to go under the radar of labour laws and regulations (Otis, 2011). For example, in Waterfall Restaurant, none of the performers have signed employment contracts in any form. They only have the restaurant owner's verbal agreement to allow them to work there. This is against labour laws in China and therefore illegal. However, local governments often have less incentive to strictly implement labour laws while trying to keep labour costs low in order to attract investment and develop local economies (Friedman and Lee, 2010; Lin and Mao, 2022b). Migrant workers as 'outsiders' also have fewer resources and networks to enable them to assert their labour rights. Also, unlike workers in factories who can take collective action such as strikes (with success in some cases) (see, for example, Chan and Pun, 2009; Hui and Chan, 2022), collective action does not seem like an option for service workers in small-scale businesses. Therefore, performers work in a context where the business owner has the power to define labour conditions and workplace rules on his or her own terms.

The restaurant owner of Waterfall Restaurant is a middle-aged woman, and everyone calls her Ms Yang. Before restaurant workers commence employment, they need to hand in photocopies of their identity cards, as well as a deposit of 1,000 yuan (roughly 100 pounds sterling) to Ms Yang, which is half of one month's wage. The purpose is to discipline workers and prevent them from leaving the job without the permission of Ms Yang. Such procedures are illegal but not uncommon in China, especially for migrant workers. If a worker quits without Ms Yang's approval, they lose the deposit money. As a consequence, when workers want to change jobs, they risk losing their deposit money, which is not a small sum for them considering their wage.

Moreover, it is notoriously difficult to take time off from Waterfall Restaurant other than the normal, weekly day off, which is in fact only a half day per week for each worker. There is also a rule that a worker can only take extra time off four times a year, under circumstances that are approved by Ms Yang, and two workers cannot take leave at the same time.

Therefore, leave time is not a guaranteed right for workers but a luxury. They have to carefully calculate and manage their opportunities for taking leave, and also need to negotiate this with other workers because there can only be one person taking leave at a time. This sometimes creates tensions between workers, since conflicts may arise when they are negotiating this. Therefore, such working conditions create a situation in which, on the one hand, performers are expected to create intimacy at guests' banqueting tables by undertaking multiple types of work, and, on the other hand, their own spaces for intimacy – such as spending time with family or friends, or having good relationships with co-workers – are largely compromised.

To sum up, migrant performers, like many other rural–urban migrants, are working in precarious jobs without much employment protection. They work without signing an employment contract with business owners, and such practices are tolerated by the local labour bureaus since the need to develop the local economy takes priority over the labourers' rights. The lack of a labour contract and formal regulations means that workers are much more prone to exploitation and unreasonable treatment. The business owner has too much power, and she or he becomes the sole rule-maker in terms of the working policies and regulations. It also creates a labour context that 'allows customers to exert direct control over, and often dominate, workers' (Otis, 2011: 4), as managers will side with customers but not with the workers, even if they are treated unfairly by the customers. Such a context ensures that migrant workers are not only economically vulnerable, but also emotionally exploited.

It is in this context that one can see the intersection of labour, mobility, and capital, which creates the proliferation of borders and border struggles. In the following section, I will seek to describe some of the intimate negotiations that performers have to make when encountering these bordering processes.

Intimate border encounters

The need to constantly encounter different forms of borders through daily work and migration is emotionally demanding and has an effect on performers' sense of self and their relationships with others. Such intimate border encounters will be demonstrated through the following two examples, that is, performers' sense of entitlement to respect, and their off-work entertainment.

Sense of entitlement to respect

Working in the restaurant as a waitress was a new experience for me, and the first thing I noticed was how customers treated me in a very different way to how other people treat me when they regard me as a well-educated, urban, middle-class person. There was one instance when I realized a customer had left her coat in the restaurant, and I ran to the parking lot to hand her the coat. I was shocked as she just took the coat from me and left without saying anything. That is why I did not feel surprised when there was a heated debate online in 2019 in China about whether people should say 'thank you' to delivery workers, since a survey showed that being thanked when making deliveries is among the top three concerns for delivery workers; yet workers barely receive 'thanks' when they deliver the goods (What's on Weibo, 2019). It was through numerous encounters with customers that I realized how I had taken for granted the level of respect and social recognition that had been shown to me for many years. The moment I started to dress like an ethnic performer undertaking a migrant's job, I was immediately subject to a different level of respect and social recognition. Such an experience also enabled me to have greater empathy with my informants, as I experienced first-hand how it is not easy, and full of ambivalence, to constantly experience such encounters and bordering during everyday work.

For example, I remember vividly a situation when I was working with a waitress named Fang at Waterfall Restaurant. As she and I were setting up the dinner table while waiting for the guests to arrive, she looked at the full table of delicate dishes and said to me: "You know, sometimes I wonder when could I ever afford to have such a feast? I don't think I will ever be able to do that." I know that Fang is probably right, since one such feast would cost more than half of her monthly wage. In *Factory Girls*, Leslie Chang (2009) writes about how women migrant workers who work in a factory to produce luxury handbags and purses would rarely have the opportunity to see how the end product (for example a Gucci bag) was used and enjoyed by customers in the countries of the Global North. A drastically different dynamic applies to performers' work, as their close interactions with customers are both the labour and the end product of their service work (see Figure 2.4). The inequalities, both materially and emotionally, experienced by performers though such service encounters are incredibly stark and straightforward.

It is not just the increasingly widening economic gap that is experienced by service workers like Fang during their daily working lives, but also the emotional gap regarding what they feel they are entitled to – for example, respect. For instance, an informant named Jiang talked about how it was normal for her to put up with guests' unreasonable requests and their bad temper during work. She shared how some drunk customers would deliberately spill the money on the floor when paying and watch her get down to pick the money up. When sharing these incidents, Jiang did not show any anger. Instead, she said, "As a migrant worker, it is inevitable that you become a person whom anyone can vent his spite upon". For Jiang, being a migrant worker was immediately linked with being entitled to a

Figure 2.4: Service encounters between performers and guests. Photo taken by author.

lower level of respect. Jiang's lack of anger also reveals how such inequalities become internalized for her. In another part of the interview, she said she had ended up *dagong* (doing migrant work) because she did not have a good grade at school (*xuexi buhao*). In fact, many informants had similar answers when I asked them why they migrated to seek work. Poor academic performance was the most common answer rather than rural–urban or ethnic inequalities. Jiang, like many other informants with children, also said that her biggest wish was that her daughter would do better at school, so that she would not end up *dagong* like her mother.

It is telling how customers and workers carry within themselves different 'structures of entitlement' when they encounter each other through service work. Such 'structures of entitlement' – how people from different social groups have different senses of what they are entitled to (Hanser, 2008: 8) – relate to the micro and mundane aspects of life, such as how much respect a person expects to receive when he or she steps into service encounters. While urban guests step into service encounters with a sense of entitlement to respect, service workers like Jiang work hard to acknowledge guests' respectability while they themselves do not feel that they are entitled to the same level of respect. Here, respectability becomes a powerful way to speak about, manifest, and even reinforce class difference (Skeggs, 1997, 2004). Such a differential entitlement to respect was not only produced in the service encounters per se, it was also ensured by different institutionalized regimes, such as the migration and labour regimes discussed previously.

Working at the frontier of service work, performers experience first-hand the differential treatment between them and privileged guests on a daily basis. They cannot afford the feasting table that they are used to preparing and setting up; they do not feel that they deserve to be treated with the same amount of respect that they are required and expected to show to guests. The border is not an easy place to live, and fierce border struggles happen as migrant performers strive to be recognized as respectable and modern through their off-work consumption and entertainment – something that one cannot achieve at the workplace.

Desires to be respectable and modern: off-work consumption and entertainment

Nothing is more enjoyable than finally finishing a long day of tiring work in the restaurant. I have noticed that many informants change their clothes immediately after work, even if there is only a short walk from the restaurant to the dormitory. They seem to be eager to take off their work uniforms – colourful minority clothes that advertise their differences from most of the urban citizens and broadcast their ethnic and rural origins. Right after work, they change into their own clothes – mostly fashionable outfits, among which some are counterfeit copies of famous labels like Nike and Adidas. Some of the girls will reapply their makeup before stepping out of the restaurant. For some of the migrant workers, their time for socializing and entertainment is just starting after work.

It was at first surprising for me to find out that many of the informants spend a large amount of money on entertainment after work. Nightclubs, karaoke bars, and barbecue booths are places that they usually patronize with co-workers and friends. As they often get off work late, these socializing and entertainment activities usually happen late at night and usually end at or after midnight. I joined such entertainment activities on several occasions, trying to find out why many informants spend so much of their hard-earned wages on such activities. It is not easy to understand, since when I asked the informants about this during the interviews they often found it difficult to articulate the reasons why they enjoyed entertainment activities so much. However, many of them did complain to me that it was difficult to save money since a large part of their wages went in the consumption of clothes and entertainment.

Otis (2011) has proposed the concept of 'aspiring urbanites' to describe how migrant workers respond to their marginal position by dressing up like, and longing to become, urbanites. This mainly applies to migrant workers in the service sectors. They are in a marginal position in society because of the institutionalized regimes discussed in the previous section. These include the *hukou* system, which renders them as second-class citizens, and the absence of any legal protection of their labour, which gives too much power to customers and neglects the daily discrimination that workers experience at work. As a response, migrant workers aspire to look like or behave like urbanites in order to earn respect outside work. Other research has also shown that instead of viewing rural migrants' consumption as individualistic choices, a more sophisticated understanding should take into account the social context that shapes their consumption practices (Zheng, 2003). For migrant workers who are unable to gain power and recognition through formal channels, everyday practices, even at a superficial and trivial level, can become a form of resistance (Ding, 2017).

These theories can also help us to understand the mentality behind the informants' consumption of entertainment activities. As I have described before, migrant workers who work at the frontier of service work experience different intersecting borders during their daily lives. Many informants mentioned that entertainment is useful in terms of releasing the stress they experience at work. More importantly, during such activities they successfully transfer their roles from 'producers' to 'consumers', thus entering power relationships in which they are the more powerful side. Interestingly, some informants also associate the consumption of entertainment with the project of discipline of the self to become modern citizens by keeping up with new trends and by letting go of the 'backward' and 'country-bumpkin' self-images:

Lang:	Men are like this. They prefer to have fun. If you don't go out and have fun, you will probably be left behind. But if you play too much, that's not reasonable either.
Researcher:	Why would not going out lead you to fall behind?
Lang:	If you don't play you will become a thoughtless man. You don't have contact with other people, right? You will become dumber, and won't know how to behave properly. You just sit there looking silly. Is that a good thing for you? No! Whether what you say is right or not, be open, right? People will think you are a fun person too. (Lang, 27 years old, male, Lahu, Forest Park)

For Lang, 'knowing how to play' has become closely related to his self-identity and masculinity. He internalizes the feeling that minority people are backward and shy, and therefore need to improve themselves by practising social skills and keeping up with modern lifestyles in the city. Hence, he treats entertainment and socializing as a kind of self-improvement tool that might enable him to abandon the image of the rural, backward self and embrace the modern, open-minded self.

Besides, entertainment has become a major way for migrant workers to experience potential romance, love, and sex. Migrant male workers are usually undesirable marriage partners in the city (Sun, 2023). Their meagre wages mean that they cannot compete with male urbanites or those fellow villagers who are better off. More often than not, they are caught between the Western ideology of romance and love and the need to conform to traditional practices of marriage with local girls back home (Wang and Nehring, 2014; Choi and Peng, 2016). With migrant workers being treated as undesirable marriage partners in the cities, they use entertainment opportunities to express their longing for romance, love, and sex. In fact, many informants meet their dates or future partners during these entertainment activities.

However, such opportunities do not come without certain costs. During a later interview, Lang also mentioned the conflicting feelings he had towards socializing. On the one hand, his meagre wage does not allow him to spend much on socializing. On the other hand, he thinks women are realistic nowadays, and he feels the need to invest more in potential relationships.

Researcher: Do you think it is difficult to find a girlfriend?
Lang: It is a bit hard for us, yes. In the city, you have to spend money. You have to treat girls to meals, buy them presents, take them out to have fun, right? That's not small money if you sum it up. Otherwise, girls have other places to go. (Lang, 27 years old, male, Lahu, Forest Park)

Lang is stating that women overvalue men's financial situation, and he feels the stress in relation to his courtship practices. The practice of bill-paying is gendered in China, with men expected to pay the bill during dates to showcase their masculinity (Choi and Peng, 2016). This has added to the economic burden of dating for some migrant workers with low incomes. Sometimes, it further marginalized them in the urban marriage market. For migrant workers who do spend a lot of time and money on consumption and entertainment, this has put them in a more vulnerable position, as their financial capabilities are further weakened by such practices.

Nevertheless, this does not mean that women are the ones that benefit from such activities. Female migrant workers are sometimes stigmatized for participating in entertainment activities. There is a clear double standard towards the desirability of men and women's participation. For example, some of the male informants specifically said that they do not want their future girlfriends or spouses to spend too much time going out and having fun. Meanwhile, they seem to be fine with themselves going out quite often. This has led to disputes between couples as well, sometimes even leading to the end of relationships. This is because of an essentialized understanding of gender and the moralizing of women's sexuality, which will be further explored in Chapter 5 when examining the gendered aspects of border encounters for migrant performers.

These two examples not only illustrate how performers encounter bordering processes in emotional and personal ways, but also show the blurred boundaries between their work and personal lives. The lack of respect or the sense of entitlement to be respected at work leads informants to seek respect and a sense of self-worth elsewhere. Through spending large amounts of money on consumption and entertainment activities, they aspire to add value to themselves and become respectable (Skeggs, 1997). Consumption and entertainment also become ways for them to work on their 'project of self' (Rose, 1992), so that they can aspire to be urban, modern citizens who know their way around and are different from the backward, primitive images that they have to present at work. The borders between work and life are thereby challenged as well. As Kathi Weeks powerfully states in her article 'Life within and against work':

> Once we recognize that work produces subjects, the borders that would contain it are called into question. It is not only that work and life cannot be confined to particular sites, from the perspective of the production of subjectivity, work and life are thoroughly interpenetrated. The subjectivities shaped at work do not remain at work but inhabit all the spaces and times of non-work and vice-versa. Who one becomes at work and in life are mutually constitutive. There is no position of exteriority in this sense; work is clearly part of life and life part of work. (Weeks, 2007: 246)

In that sense, these two examples – the sense of entitlement at work in relation to respect, and after work consumption and entertainment – are certainly interrelated as well. It is difficult to spot the borders between life and work, since it is difficult to say at what point work stops and life begins. However, there are other forms of borders that profoundly shape people's emotions, senses of self, and relationships. Since such borders are intimately and emotionally experienced by performers in this research, intimacy as a lens provides us with valuable perspectives to further explore the meanings of borders.

Conclusion: life, work, and intimate borders

In this chapter I have provided a detailed description of what performers' work is like. By exploring the meaning of ethnic performance, and by theorizing it through sociological concepts, I firstly discussed why work is a useful starting point of inquiry, and therefore deserves further theorization.

Furthermore, by showing how a single framework cannot capture the multidimensional meaning of ethnic performance, and as the multiplication of labour means that performers are expected to do several kinds of work at the same time, this chapter argues that ethnic performance could be best theorized as a site of encounters. This, on the one hand, means that the service encounter between performers and customers, due to the nature of interactive service work, requires that they interact with each other in a physically proximate manner. On the other hand, ethnic performance is also a site where performers have to constantly encounter multiple bordering processes at the same time. Such encounters are intimate, personal, and emotional – as shown through the examples of performers' senses of entitlement to respect and their consumption and entertainment activities. These intimate encounters with borders also point to the need to see work and personal life as closely related and mutually constitutive, rather than different spheres with clear boundaries.

This chapter lays a foundation for later chapters in theorizing the usefulness of the lens of intimacy to understand these border struggles and border encounters. Further, as I have shown in this chapter, these bordering processes most prominently revolve around the rural–urban divide, ethnicity, and gender. Therefore, in the following three chapters I will discuss in more detail performers' experiences of border encounters through work and migration. As the performers are firstly and foremostly rural–urban migrants, the rural–urban divide is something they have to encounter during their everyday lives. Hence, the next chapter will illustrate the intimate negotiations migrant performers must make with respect to the rural–urban border. The lens of intimacy will be used to understand these border struggles in relation to the rural–urban divide.

3

Intimate Negotiations along Rural–Urban Borders

Introduction

During the Spring Festival of 2017, I went to a friend's home in a rural village. It was two days before the Lunar New Year, and the road was busy with traffic as many people were travelling home for this special occasion – rural–urban migrants were also among these travellers. One image attracted my attention, and it still lingers in my memory vividly today. It was a man who was riding a motorcycle and from the way he dressed, he looked like one of the migrant workers who was driving home. What attracted me was a box of fruit attached to the back of the motorcycle. On the box there were three big Chinese characters – *Zhongguo Meng* (The China Dream). It looked like a gift he had bought for his family back home, as it is common to bring gifts home during Spring Festival. The man with the motorcycle travelled past our car quickly, but the three big characters lingered in my mind for a while.

The China Dream is a slogan coined by President Xi Jinping in 2013, which underlines China's national goal of furthering its powerful role on the world stage. Needless to say, urbanization is also part of this big dream, as are the hundreds of millions of migrant workers behind this dream. The China Dream also emphasizes securing the happiness of the people, and ties this goal closely with the advancing of China as a nation. It could be said that rural–urban migration has become a means for many rural people to fulfil their 'China Dreams'. Indeed, when informants were talking about their reasons for migrating, they rarely regarded economic reasons as the sole or most important driver that motivated them. Their migration journeys were motivated by complex emotions that were shaped by certain imaginaries and aspirations related to being good citizens and living good lives – such as that depicted by the China Dream. The image of the man carrying the fruit box struck me not just because of the emotions it evoked for me as a researcher, but also as a reminder of the need to put emotions at the centre of inquiry to understand rural–urban migrants' experiences.

This chapter demonstrates how the lens of intimacy enables us to understand ethnic performers' experiences of the rural–urban divide as fundamentally emotional, and what we can learn from taking a closer look at these emotional experiences. Without confining the emotional to the relationship sphere, in this chapter I will ask questions such as what migration regimes make people feel, and how the emotions people have when experiencing such migration regimes reveal the underlying assumptions and working mechanisms of such administrative bordering.

The first section of this chapter brings emotions into theorizing rural–urban migration, in particular the role of *hukou* as a form of administrative border in producing and sustaining the rural–urban divide. Taking informants' complex emotional reflexivity regarding *hukou* seriously will help to illuminate 'the *hukou* puzzle' (Chen and Fan, 2016) – why migrants are not enthusiastic about transferring their *hukou* to the urban area where they work and live, despite lacking a local *hukou* makes their lives difficult in many ways. Taking account of emotions helps to provide alternative understandings rather than assuming migrants are making such decisions merely based on rational choices. It also reveals the underlying assumptions of *hukou*, and how individuals' emotions reveal the broader emotional regime of our time.

Besides, *hukou* is just one among the many forms of bordering that shapes the rural–urban divide. The bordering process also works through attaching different cultural meanings to the rural and the urban. Such different value systems shape migrants' personhood by motivating them to embrace migration in order to achieve valuable personhood. It is an example of how borders produce and shape subjectivities in different ways, and how the bordering relies on the administrative, the symbolic, and the cultural to produce differential inclusion (Mezzadra and Neilson, 2013). This chapter shows the value of using intimacy as a lens to understand migrant performers' experience of encountering the rural–urban divide.

Bringing emotions into theorizing rural–urban migration in China

While the notion of emotions and migration has become a burgeoning field of study (Svasek and Skrbis, 2007; Ahmed, 2010; Boccagni and Baldassar, 2015), it remains a neglected area in the Chinese context. Emotions are never absent from rural–urban migration processes: the loneliness and fragmented lives workers endure in factories; the anger and sadness of being marginalized and being looked down upon; the alienation of living and working under exploitative conditions; the heartbreak of separation from their 'left-behind children'; but also the pleasure of going out and seeing the world (see, for example, Jacka, 2012; Zhou et al, 2014; Pun, 2016). These all point to the emotional nature of migration. However, little research has placed emotion at the centre of inquiry when considering how rural–urban migration makes people feel. The idea of emotion is scattered throughout the literature on rural–urban migration rather than being systematically organized and analyzed. And in the few notable exceptions that take emotions seriously (Wang and Nehring, 2014; Choi and Peng, 2016; Sun, 2023), they are usually theorized within the sphere of intimate relationships. Without diminishing the importance of such a focus, it is beneficial to broaden the scope of this inquiry and ask further questions about how such migration regimes make people feel.

Despite the fact that it is notoriously difficult to define emotions, the theorization of migration would benefit from a closer engagement with sociological theories of emotions. For example, different definitions of emotions would influence the different theoretical approaches that could be used to research emotions and migration. In this chapter, I largely draw on emotion theories such as emotional reflexivity (Holmes, 2010; Brownlie, 2011; Burkitt, 2012) and emotional regime (Reddy, 2001) to help make sense of people's emotions in relation to migration.

Sociologists of emotions have long argued against the tendency to see emotions as entities within individuals' minds and bodies. Instead, it is necessary to see emotions as relational, that is, as they emerge and evolve in relation to other people and in relation to certain contexts. I follow Burkitt's theory in defining emotion as a response to the way in which people are embedded in patterns of relationship, both to others and to significant social and political events or situations (Burkitt, 2014). I also find the concept of 'emotional experience' useful in that it allows us to talk about complex emotions without necessarily naming the emotional categories that we are referring to (McKenzie, 2016), such as positive and negative emotions, or happiness and unhappiness. According to McKenzie (2016: 50), to explore 'emotional experience' is to recognize 'the emotional dimensions of social experience', and to 'reinforce the function of emotion as an experience that connects the self to society as mutually dependent concepts'. This also reaffirms the insight that both emotion and emotional experiences are deeply embedded in patterns of social relationships. Therefore, by using emotion as a lens to understand performers' experience of encountering the rural–urban border, the broader social context that shapes such encounters will need to be revealed. It is difficult to specify when and where these encounters happen, as borders proliferate in many different aspects of social life (Mezzadra and Neilson, 2013). However, it is necessary to acknowledge the fact that the encountering of the rural–urban divide can happen in many different contexts for rural–urban migrants, including encountering the urban landscape, interacting with other people, and so on. It can also happen not just in real-life encounters, but also in migrants' imaginaries as they think about their future plans and their entitlements as migrants. Among all these invisible borders that characterize the rural–urban divide, *hukou* policy is definitely a prominent one, and arguably a more or less formal bordering mechanism. Therefore, my examination of performers' emotional encounters with rural–urban borders will start there.

Encountering rural–urban bordering through the formal system of *hukou*

When one thinks of the borders that divide and define the rural and the urban in China, the first thing to note is probably the administrative border of the *hukou* system. *Hukou* has also long been at the centre of the debate on rural–urban migration in China. It classifies people into agricultural *hukou* and non-agricultural *hukou* according to their place of birth. Although this division between agricultural and non-agricultural *hukou* is starting to vanish in many places in China, the division between local and non-local remains. As *hukou* continues to curtail internal migrants' access to welfare provisions and public services such as housing, medical care, and education, rural migrants without local *hukou* continue to be excluded and marginalized in various ways, especially in big cities with stringent population control (Dong and Goodburn, 2020). Therefore, the system of *hukou* still plays a significant role in constructing the rural–urban divide and further contributing to the class formation of Chinese society.

The following section firstly outlines one of the surprises that puzzled me when I found out that informants are generally not willing to transfer their *hukou* to Green City, although they can do so in theory. Responding to an article which systematically examined this '*hukou* puzzle' (Chen and Fan, 2016), I argue for the need to take into account the role of emotions in understanding this puzzle. I further explore what kinds of emotions are involved during migrants' negotiations around their sense of entitlement to local *hukou,* and how 'emotional reflexivity' can be a useful concept here to understand their negotiations over *hukou*. Meanwhile, the concept of emotional regime (Reddy, 2001) will be used to understand these emotions in relation to their broader social and historical context: neoliberal governance in China.

The hukou *puzzle*

While it is well-recognized that migrants without *hukou* are rendered vulnerable in different ways (Solinger, 1999; Liang, 2016; Lin and Mao, 2022a), it is often implied that urban *hukou* ought to be a desirable status for migrants to achieve, since the absence of a local *hukou* contributes to migrants' own exclusion and marginalization. Therefore, it was initially surprising for me to learn that most of my informants were not as enthusiastic to transfer their *hukou* to Green City as I expected them to be. The same surprise has been increasingly shared by other scholars, although it remains under-theorized.

Chen and Fan's (2016) article is among the first which systematically explores this puzzle by asking why rural migrants do not want urban *hukou* (hereafter the '*hukou* puzzle'). Relying on the Floating Population Dynamic Monitoring Survey (2010–2012), which sampled 4,912 residents' committees and villages in 106 cities nation-wide using probability proportional to size sampling, Chen and Fan (2016) explore how migrant workers respond to changing *hukou* policies, and the rationales underlying their decision-making in relation to *hukou* transfer. The changing value of urban *hukou* and rural *hukou* is at the core of their theorization. To be more specific, they argue that with the increasing benefits attached to rural *hukou*, the value gap between rural *hukou* and urban *hukou* is increasingly diminished. Migrants in many places no longer need to obtain urban *hukou* in order to access many basic social rights – for example their children's right to education. As transferring *hukou* means losing the right to use rural land in most cases, maintaining rural land back home becomes the most important answer to the *hukou* puzzle. Therefore, migrants are motivated to 'straddle the city and countryside in order to maximise their entitlements and minimise risks' (Chen and Fan, 2016: 31).

Undoubtedly, Chen and Fan's article is among the first to bridge the theoretical gap of the *hukou* puzzle, and convincing evidence and arguments are provided to try to make sense of the puzzle. However, firstly, what this theorizing lacks is the perspectives and voices of the migrants themselves. While the big data set is useful in revealing overall patterns, it cannot speak for people's own experiences. Secondly, the underlying assumption of Chen and Fan's theorization is that migrants have all the knowledge they need to make these decisions. However, as shown through my fieldwork, migrants do not always have all the information they need to make *hukou* transfer decision as a result of the fast-changing *hukou* policies, as well as their outsider status. Thirdly, the underlying assumption that people will always make rational choices in order to maximize their profits largely neglects how emotions play important roles in these negotiations. There is a lot more to consider when migrants are making decisions about *hukou* transfer, such as their relationships with significant others, how they envision their entitlements, and what aspirations they have for their future lives. Therefore, considering *hukou* transfer is not just about rationally calculated gains and losses, but is fundamentally an emotional experience. It has already been pointed out that migrants do not make decisions regarding whether to stay in the city based solely on rationality, as emotion plays a major role in their decision-making process (Du and Li, 2012). In the following sections, I show how we can understand the *hukou* puzzle differently by taking into account different emotions that infuse migrants' encountering of *hukou* as an administrative border.

Hukou *policy in Green City – an opaque and changing system*

Firstly, it is important to situate 'the *hukou* puzzle' in its local context, as *hukou* policies are very different in different areas. The *hukou* system in China has changed over time, with gradual changes over the past 30 years loosening the rigid controls over population mobility (Liang, 2016). The so-called '*hukou* reform' in 2014 was intended to abolish the division between agricultural and non-agricultural *hukou*. However, the reform was far from thorough, since the long-existing division between local and non-local *hukou* still remains (Goodburn, 2014). Along with the *hukou* reform, another change that has occurred is that, since the 1990s, local governments have had more power and autonomy in dictating the implementation of their *hukou* policies, whereas the power was largely in the hands of the central government previously (Chan and Buckingham, 2008). However, as Guo and Liang (2017) rightly remind us, although local governments' autonomy in deciding *hukou* policies is not without restriction, *hukou* policies can nevertheless be implemented quite differently in different places.

More importantly, the implementation of *hukou* policy in small- and medium-sized cities can be quite different from big cities like Beijing and Shanghai. Some literature suggests that *hukou* conversion – transferring one's *hukou* to the city – is easier in small- to medium-sized cities because local governments may have less to offer in terms of public services and welfare provision (Chan and Buckingham, 2008; Tao, 2010). In fact, small- and medium-sized cities are purportedly at the forefront of the *hukou* reform (Tao, 2010; Goodburn, 2014; Zhang, 2018). There are also attempts to bring in new procedures to enable migrants to transfer their *hukou* to the cities. For example, the point-based system, which is similar to some countries' immigration systems, has been utilized by more and more cities in China to select the few, eligible migrants and grant them local *hukou* (see Dong and Goodburn, 2020). Such selections are largely based on migrants' 'personal qualities', such as educational levels, whether they are in formal employment, and so on. Therefore, the primary aim is to develop local economies by attracting 'talent', rather than promoting social equity. Most migrant workers are not qualified for point-based migration, since they are not usually highly educated, and they tend to take up informal employment (Lin, 2015); indeed, in this research the migrant performers who work as service workers in small restaurants and tourist sites fall into this category. The point-based system, therefore, creates further inequality among migrant groups, and there is still a big gap between citizens' demand and state provision (Guo and Liang, 2017; Dong and Goodburn, 2020).

More recent literature confirms that a differentiated approach to *hukou* acquisition (*chabiehua luohu*) was implemented in 2014 to allow cities of different sizes to have different *hukou* policy principles (State Council, 2014, cited in Zhang, 2018). Among them, the policy principles for towns and small cities (county-level cities) are that '*hukou* acquisition should be open to all those with legal and stable residence' (Zhang, 2018: 866). Such policy shifts call for more empirical data about how migrants themselves experience the loosening *hukou* policies in small- and medium-sized cities, which remains a relatively under-researched area. Therefore, Green City provides a good example for study, as it is a small city in Southwest China with a population of around 300,000, and is not a popular migration destination compared to many big cities in the eastern coastal areas. One might wonder, therefore, whether migration regimes like *hukou* are implemented differently there, and what it means for migrants like my informants.

As reported in the news media,[1] some local governments were even encouraging people to switch their *hukou* from agricultural to non-agricultural, since they were under pressure from the central government to achieve certain quotas to increase the percentage of the urban population (as the number was often used to measure urbanization). The process was often called *nongzhuancheng* (from rural to urban). Therefore, certain local governments were even pushing villagers who remained in the villages to transfer their *hukou* to the city in order to meet the requirement of this quota. On the government website of Green City, I found multiple documents at the provincial level urging the local governments to meet certain targets of *hukou* transference.[2] I suspect that at a certain point, the Green City government was subject to pressure to achieve a certain target for purposes of achieving bureaucratic goals. Overall, the *hukou* policy in Green City and the ways it was implemented were more nuanced and complicated than the rather homogeneous depiction of *hukou* in most migration literature would suggest.

Generally, without interviewing local government officials, I have little knowledge of how the *hukou* policy was implemented in Green City. The fact that I was not easily able to learn about these policies is a clear indication that the *hukou* system is an opaque one, which makes it even more difficult for migrants to navigate as outsiders without local networks. When Chen and Fan (2016) argue that migrants are making rational choices in order to maximize their benefits, the underlying assumption is that people have enough information to weigh their gains and losses, which is not what I have found in this research. As people are navigating an opaque migration system, the role of emotions is even more important, and therefore should not be neglected.

Emotional reflexivity in making hukou *transfer decisions*

The concept of 'emotional reflexivity' is particularly useful in shedding light on how emotions are always involved in shaping the ways migrants experience *hukou*.

Reflexivity – the capacity of humans to make sense of their lives based on existing knowledge – is often defined as rational and based on calculation. It tends to be regarded as disembodied individuals stepping away from their emotions and rationally considering their situation based on existing knowledge (Giddens, 1991). However, existing literature has convincingly shown how it is necessary to bring emotions into the theorization of reflexivity (Holmes, 2010; Brownlie, 2011; Burkitt, 2012). Emotional reflexivity is not a complete departure from the normative definition of reflexivity, but it points to the need to bring the emotional angle into understanding reflexivity. Therefore, the rational and emotional are inseparable in understanding reflexivity. In that sense, reflexivity can be defined as 'an emotional, embodied and cognitive process in which social actors have feelings about and try to understand and alter their lives in relation to their social and natural environment and to others' (Holmes, 2010: 140). Reflexivity is emotional also due to the ways that emotions are 'woven into the fabric of the interactions we are engaged in', and emotional reflexivity 'is therefore also central to the way we relate to ourselves as well as to others' (Burkitt, 2012: 459). Therefore, by using emotional reflexivity to think about informants' decision-making processes regarding *hukou*, it is crucial to understand how their emotions are deeply situated and shaped by their relations and interactions with others and with their social surroundings.

I define emotional reflexivity as the ways that emotions are always involved in shaping the ways people think about their positions in the social world, and take actions accordingly. I find this concept useful because when people are making decisions about *hukou*, they are actually thinking about something bigger than that, for example, their life stage, sense of belonging, how they define success and happiness, and their aspirations and desires. In other words, they are thinking about their own personhood, their relationships with other people, and their relationships with their social world. The following quotes are examples:

> 'If I could finally start my own business and be successful, of course I would want to transfer my *hukou* here and stay in Green City permanently. Who doesn't, really? But I would not dare to think about things this far ahead … It's useless to think about success and *hukou* and things like that when you are nowhere near it. The best thing to do is to focus on your current life, and try your best to succeed.' (Yang, 23 years old, male, Han, Waterfall Restaurant)

'I will probably think about transferring my *hukou* when I get married and settle down. Before that, it makes no sense to do so. I am the only daughter in my family. I cannot carry my *hukou* wherever I go, right?' (Ping, 25 years old, female, Lahu, Forest Park)

Firstly, these two quotes are typical in showing how young migrants usually consider *hukou* transfer decisions in relation to their life stages. While male informants like Yang often attach *hukou* with having one's own successful career, female informants like Ping often attach *hukou* with marriage and settling down. Therefore, the *hukou* decision is also very much about what kinds of people they envision themselves to be, their relationships with other people, and the future lives they aspire to live. To think about *hukou* largely requires emotional reflexivity. Indeed, there are different emotions infused with this process.

A sense of shame was shown through Yang's remarks, as he does not think that he deserves to get an urban *hukou* since he is not successful at the moment. 'Not dare to think about things this far ahead' also suggests that getting *hukou* is something distant, out of reach, and could even be emotionally daunting. Informants like Yang tend to internalize that *hukou* is only for those who are successful and established, as they are already accustomed to the mentality that some forms of citizenship in China are a reward rather than something equally accessible to every citizen (Woodman and Guo, 2017). Therefore, they do not feel entitled to it, and they blame themselves for not being successful enough to gain it.

At the same time, these emotions could be understood in relation to migrants' sense of entitlement. It is crucial to recognize how people from different social positions may have different senses of what they should be entitled to. Negotiations around a sense of entitlement are inherently emotional. Hanser (2008: 8) has insightfully proposed the concept of 'structure of entitlement' to understand how people from different class backgrounds have different senses of entitlement, and carry such different senses of entitlement with them into social interactions. The imaginary sense of entitlement matters, as research has shown how different kinds of cultural qualifications shape how migrants imagine their entitlement to *hukou*, for example, migrants with higher educational levels think they deserve local *hukou*, and they take that sense of entitlement for granted (Woodman, 2017). Moreover, Yang's reflection on himself as not being successful at the moment also shows how his definition of 'successful' is largely shaped by the hegemonic masculinity ideal which closely relates one's masculinity with money-earning abilities (Choi and Peng, 2016; Choi, 2018).

What Ping says also reveals the underlying logic of *hukou* which regards sedentarism as the norm, and problematizes the settlement of people who are constantly mobile (Salazar and Schiller, 2014; Woodman and Guo, 2017). 'I cannot carry my *hukou* everywhere' is a common dilemma facing all migrants who might be constantly on the move. It means that it is difficult, if not impossible, for one to obtain a local *hukou* wherever they go. As *hukou* fundamentally works as a mechanism that ties a person's welfare entitlement to a certain place, it is a system that normalizes sedentarism. Allowing migrants to transfer their *hukou* from rural areas to urban areas cannot fundamentally solve the problem unless the *hukou* system is abolished completely. Ping's remarks also highlight the relational aspect of emotional reflexivity (Holmes, 2010; Burkitt, 2012), as she reflected on her position as the 'only daughter' in the family and her relationship with her parents when considering *hukou* decisions, rather than calculating her gain and loss as an autonomous individual. In China's context, migration is usually a family strategy rather than an individual choice. The importance of the family and the strong social norm of filial piety clearly inform Ping's emotional reflexivity, coupled with the gendered socio-cultural norms which expect migrant women to shoulder more caring responsibilities (Murphy, 2008). These aspects point to the need to understand emotional reflexivity in its local context, considering how various social and cultural norms differently inform the particular nature of emotional reflexivity.

Secondly, even though having one's *hukou* transferred to Green City is theoretically easy according to the policies discussed earlier, in practice it remains difficult to achieve. Such difficulty mainly comes from the lack of information on how *hukou* actually works for many informants. None of my informants seemed to know about how things worked exactly in Green City, and information about *hukou* seemed to be inaccessible for the majority of them. As mentioned before, even as a researcher I could not gather enough information about how the *hukou* policy worked in Green City unless I talked to government officials. It could be argued that the *hukou* system is quite opaque in Green City, as opposed to the clearly structured systems, such as the points-based system, in many other cities. Migrants' outsider status makes it especially difficult for them to access such information, as they are less likely to have local networks and connections. Furthermore, with the *hukou* policy changing constantly, it is even more difficult to keep up to date with the latest versions of it. Moreover, one cannot know exactly what kinds of benefits one would lose if one's *hukou* was transferred to another place. These all contribute to a sense of uncertainty and a fear of losing out.

For example, some informants mentioned the ways that social policies regarding land are changing rapidly. They therefore have to be very careful when making decisions, or risk losing the few benefits that they have. The fear of losing out was amplified when a proper social security system was lacking:

Researcher: Have you thought about transferring your *hukou* to Green City?

Zhang: I haven't thought about it before. If you do transfer your *hukou* here, the lands back home will no longer be yours, and then you will have nothing left. If I don't have a proper job here ... I do not dare to do this. I need to at least properly settle here, and have some kind of security (*baozhang*).

Researcher: What if you did have such security here?

Zhang: If that were the case ... I think ... I would want to transfer *hukou* here. I wanted to have my mother moved here ... I mean move to live here. Because back home ... I feel sad when thinking about how hard my mom has to work. (Zhang, 19 years old, male, Hani, Waterfall Restaurant)

Zhou: I need to think about my children – if I have no land left for them, what will they do if they can't survive in the city in the future? ... Everything is changing so fast in this society ... The road leading to the Park, it used to be a muddy road ... Who knows what the future may bring? (Zhou, 40 years old, female, Hani, Tea Park)

Echoing Zhang and Zhou, other informants were reluctant to consider *hukou* transfer because of their entitlements to land. At the same time, children's education is the primary issue that motivates migrants to transfer their *hukou* to the city. These findings echo what has been revealed by large data sets (see Chen and Fan, 2016). However, it is still necessary to understand a series of emotional negotiations around the right to land. Maintaining the right to use the land back home can provide a feeling of security exactly because of the lack of comprehensive social security for rural residents.

In China, there is a large gap between urban pension schemes and rural pension schemes, with the former being much more generous than the latter. Without a comprehensive rural pension scheme, rural residents still rely heavily on their land, on family support, as well as on private commercial insurance to maintain their security in old age (Shi, 2006; Lin and Nguyen, 2021). At the same time, the regional inequality of social provision is also stark in China (Shi, 2017), meaning that while rich regions may have good pension schemes for local citizens, poverty-stricken regions may have very limited pension schemes or may not have any rural pension schemes at all. Therefore, the fact that most migrants are expected to rely on themselves to arrange old-age security amplifies their fear of making the wrong decision, which would lead to detrimental consequences.

Meanwhile, since migrant workers who are not 'locals' are usually excluded from local social welfare schemes (Tao and Xu, 2007; Shi, 2017), their land remains a safety net to fall back on if they cannot successfully remain in the cities. Giving up rural *hukou* largely means giving up the right to use rural land, and as there is no system in place to fairly remunerate people for giving up their land rights (see Tao and Xu, 2007), giving up rural land for urban *hukou* is often too big a risk to take.

Thirdly, some informants are not willing to transfer their *hukou* because they do not think they belong in Green City.

Researcher:	Have you considered transferring your *hukou* to Green City?
Liang:	No. Why do that? I don't want to become a Green City person anyway. I think my hometown is a good place ... And I'm a rural person after all [*benlai jiushi nongcun ren*]. (Liang, 25 years old, male, Wa, Forest Park)

Informants like Liang mentioned that they did not wish to transfer *hukou* because they did not think of themselves as Green City people, or even urbanites. For that reason, the emotions attached to migrant workers place-identity negotiations should be recognized when trying to understand their decisions around *hukou* transfer. When their state-endorsed place-identity – manifested by *hukou* registration – confronts their individual sense of home-place, this tension makes them feel more strongly about who they are, and which place they choose to call home. From Liang's perspective, we can also see how *hukou* actively plays a role in constructing home-place-identity. Some migrants do associate the place of *hukou* registration with their home-place identity. In a sense, it could be argued that the existence of the *hukou* system makes place-based identity more salient. At the same time, the difficulty of feeling a sense of belonging in Green City also prevents informants from taking the next step towards settling down there. Rather, it reinforces their sense of being 'out of place'.

In summary, rather than understanding migrants' juggling between the rural and the urban as a way to maximize their profits, it is important to recognize the important role of emotions in this process. I am not arguing that migrants are making decisions purely based on their emotions. Instead, emotions infuse migrants' decision-making in relation to *hukou*, or how they imagine their future decisions to play out. Hence, emotional reflexivity is a useful concept here to capture the ways that emotions are always involved in informants' reflexivity regarding *hukou* decisions. Moreover, emotional reflexivity reveals how migrants' consideration of *hukou* is closely related to their senses of self, relationships with other people, and relationships with the social world in which they live. As one's emotional reflexivity is clearly situated in the broader social context, a further question needs to be asked – are there broader emotional regimes which shape people's emotional reflexivity? It is with this consideration in mind that I turn to explore the broader emotional regime in situating migrants' emotional reflexivity.

The intersection between the emotional regime and the migration regime

'Emotional regime' refers to 'a normative order for emotions', which is often enforced by political institutions in a given historical context (Reddy, 2001: 129). Elias's work on changing standards of etiquette and the emotions involved could be utilized as an example to show that there are different emotional regimes across historical and societal contexts (Elias, 1978). While Reddy's work mainly points to the overall emotional regime in a certain society as a singular form of norm (Plamper, 2010), Wettergren's work shows how organizations can embody certain emotional regimes which might be different from other institutions (Wettergren, 2010). There are emotional sub-regimes existing in one particular historical context, and certain emotions can be used to challenge the existing emotional (sub)regime (Wettergren, 2009). Therefore, the meaning of 'emotional regime' is still under negotiation.

It has been rightly pointed out that the intersection between the emotional regime and the migration regime needs further exploration, as it shapes how migrants regulate their emotional expressions in the context of transnational migration (Ho, 2014). Borrowing this idea, I employ the concept of emotional regime to refer to a set of rules, norms, and practices about how to feel within certain historical and social contexts, and situate migrant performers' experiences in the broader emotional regime of contemporary China.

Then how could we describe China's current emotional regime? I argue that the current emotional regime is deeply rooted in China's neoliberal governance, which expects people to be self-reliant. Although there is a lot of debate around the meaning of neoliberalism in China (see, for example, Harvey, 2005; Kipnis, 2007; Zhou et al, 2019), it is increasingly recognized that neoliberal ideology is used as a form of governance to shape individuals' subjectivities and emotions (Rofel, 2007; Yang, 2014; Wielander and Hird, 2018). Here, I take neoliberalism to mean how an 'individual is held responsible and accountable for his or her own actions and well-being' (Harvey, 2005: 65). This resonates with previous literature which points to the direct link between neoliberal governance in China and the discourse of *suzhi* and happiness (Yang, 2014).

Suzhi is generally translated as 'human quality', which is used in the various governing processes in China, and is also widely used in daily life (Kipnis, 2006). *Suzhi* discourse was often related to neoliberal governmentality, since they share a similar deployment of value coding which 'inscribes, measures, and mobilises human subjectivity as the powerhouse for productivity and development' (Yan 2003: 497). In that sense, some people are regarded as embodying high *suzhi*, while others are deemed as embodying low *sushi* – rural–urban migrants and ethnic minority people are often related with the latter (see, for example, Friedman, 2006; Jacka, 2009). Furthermore, *suzhi* is often used to legitimate inequality by suggesting that people are responsible for their own predicament (Murphy, 2004).

Besides, 'the quest for happiness is one of the most important stories in China today' (Kleinman et al, 2011: 267). Indeed, many mainstream discourses that characterize contemporary socialist China are to do with happiness, such as 'positive energy'(*zhengnengliang*) and 'the China Dream' (Hird, 2018). Happiness is also used by the socialist state to measure its degree of success or, so to speak, the realization of its China dream (Wielander, 2018). Under the current emotional regime characterized by neoliberal governance, the 'happiness duty' (Ahmed, 2010) falls upon the migrants themselves. As Ahmed explains:

> The happiness for migrants means telling a certain story about your arrival as good, or the good of your arrival. The happiness duty is a positive duty to speak of what is good but can also be thought of as a negative duty not to speak of what is not good, not to speak from or out of unhappiness. (Ahmed, 2010: 158)

Such 'happiness duty' is also apparent in the current emotional regime in China, which shapes migrants' emotional reflexivity through promoting a form of individualistic understanding of success and happiness. Although academic work has emphasized that happiness should be viewed as relational (Holmes and Mckenzie, 2018) and that the ways in which broader social inequality shapes emotions should be recognized, in reality neoliberal society is constantly reinforcing the idea that happiness is people's own individualistic pursuit (Yang, 2014). In order to be happy, success needs to be pursued both materially and symbolically – in other words, through social status. The China Dream is about desire, about depicting what kind of life people should aspire to, and also the attempt to relate individuals' desires to the broader project of nation-building. In that sense, happiness could also be 'effectively employed as a neoliberal technology of governance' (Yang, 2014: 39).

In line with the state's emphasis on the importance of being happy and embodying 'positive energy', as well as the ideology of 'the China Dream', migrants need to adopt emotional management to re-frame their negative emotions as positive ones. Although the sociology of emotions has challenged the dualism between 'positive emotions' and 'negative emotions', as even 'negative emotions' have positive meanings under certain circumstances (see, for example, Cieslik, 2015), the current emotional regime in China deliberately encourages this clearly divided way of understanding emotions as either positive or negative. For example, as the quotes from Yang and Zhang in the last section show, instead of revealing their discontent with the unequal *hukou* regime, they frame it as part of their own individual responsibility to achieve success and then gain entitlement to full citizenship in the city. To borrow Xiang's (2021) concept of 'suspension', they suspend their subjectivity as it is related to the present, and aspire to a better future which is related to greater monetary success and more social security. However, multi-layered, institutionalized inequality means that they will have a slim chance of ever achieving this dream and being successful.

Furthermore, it is also important to note the absence of certain emotions in this process – for example, anger. While anger has the potential to bring social change (see, for example, Holmes, 2004; Pun and Lu, 2010), migrant performers as a marginalized group are not encouraged to express their anger under the current emotional regime, which largely limits individuals' or groups' space for expressing their anger or frustration over social inequality. The fact that they may not feel angry also implies how social inequality is naturalized and internalized by people in China. Therefore, most of the time, informants use positive terms, reflecting their aspirations to be successful, to frame their emotions in relation to *hukou*. The fact that they 'do not possess the language of justice, rights and entitlements that is expected of a politically informed citizen' also means that they tend to blame themselves for their current hardship and exploitation (Sun, 2013: 29; Woodman, 2017).

To conclude, in this section I have sought to emotionalize *hukou* – that is, I have tried to understand *hukou* as something migrants experience emotionally in their everyday lives. There are different kinds of emotions involved in this process, including the sense of entitlement, the sense of security and trust, and the emotions attached to the home-place. Generally, informants internalize the idea that urban *hukou* is a form of privilege that one can earn by becoming established and successful, rather than understanding it as a form of citizenship that should be equally accessible to every citizen. The current emotional regime also encourages them to re-frame their 'negative emotions' as 'positive' ones. Therefore, rather than expressing anger over the social inequalities which deprive them of the right to have full citizenship in the city, they internalize the idea that it is their own fault for not being successful enough to earn urban *hukou*. Hence, they aspire to future success, which will mainly manifest itself through monetary earning ability.

This exploration shows that the experience of the rural–urban divide cannot be fully captured when conceived as an administrative division, as it is deeply embedded in personal, everyday experiences. Meanwhile, *hukou* is not the only bordering mechanism that shapes the rural–urban distinction. The border struggle also includes the different meanings attached to the urban and the rural. In a sense, what informants desire to achieve, or aspire to become – happiness, personhood with value, respect at work – cannot be achieved by simply gaining urban *hukou*. It is with this consideration in mind that I now turn to theorize aspects other than *hukou* in the intimate struggles across the rural–urban border.

The cultural aspect of the rural–urban divide: how the border produces subjectivity

The rural–urban divide does not only manifest itself through formal rules like *hukou*, but also works through the cultural systems of value that attach different meanings to the rural and the urban. This again demonstrates how bordering is the process through which inclusion and exclusion are made and distinctions are drawn, and how the symbolic, cultural, cognitive, and emotional boundaries overlap and interact with geopolitical borders. In this section, the lens of intimacy will continue to be used to understand how borders shape subjectivity and personhood. To be more specific, I seek to show how the desire to become modern citizens motivates rural–urban migration, as performers embrace migration to try to achieve valuable personhood.

Desire, value, and the project of self: embracing migration to be modern

In China, while the urban is usually associated with being modern, the rural is often associated with backwardness (see, for example, Cohen, 1993). In such a context, rural–urban migration becomes a way for many rural people to fulfil their desire to become modern citizens. Here, it is necessary to elaborate on the meaning of desire. Rather than seeing desires as individual pursuits, they should be understood as inherently social forces (Collins, 2018) which call for the exploration of the social contexts and power relations that produce them. As is rightly pointed out, the 'desire for migration' and 'desire pursued through migration' are often closely related (Carling and Collins, 2018: 918). It is certainly true in this case, in which migrant performers desire migration and at the same time also seek to fulfil their desires through migration. Through the lens of desire, it is also possible to explore the subject-becoming of migrants as they move through different migration journeys. That is also the reason I relate desire with informants' projects of the self.

By 'project of the self', I mean the idea of working on the self as if the self is a project that needs constant reworking, improving, and managing. As Nicolas Rose argues:

> Contemporary individuals are incited to live as if making a project of themselves: they are to work on their emotional world, their domestic

and conjugal arrangements, their relations with employment and their techniques of sexual pleasure, to develop a 'style' of living that will maximise the worth of their existence to themselves. (Rose, 1992: 9)

The project of self reveals the logic of neoliberalism, in which the state governs not through direct power, but through individual choice, autonomy, and freedom (Rose, 1992; Hoffman, 2006). At the same time, the state also governs through individuals' emotions and affects (Yang, 2014), as well as their desires.

In this research, it is easy to see how informants' desire for migration is intimately linked with their desire to become modern citizens. Previous literature has pointed out how the desire to be modern has motivated rural women's migration decisions, which can only be understood 'in the context of post-Mao modernity that privileges the urban' (Gaetano, 2004: 46). The use of migration as a means to fulfil the desire of becoming modern is especially prominent for ethnic minority migrants, since the intersection of being rural and being ethnic further marginalizes them in the pursuit of modernization.

Wang was a young performer in Tea Park. Growing up in a Lahu village, Wang regarded being Lahu as an important part of his identity. At the age of 21, Wang had already migrated to several places in China, and he seemed to be proud when mentioning his extensive travel experiences to me. Being spotted by a businessman who has been to Tea Park and was impressed by Wang and his fellows' performance, Wang and four other Lahu performers were invited by the businessman to go to Shanghai to perform in an ethnic-themed restaurant. It was easy to notice the sense of pride in Wang's tone and bodily gestures when he was talking about that experience. He talked about how he and his friends managed to conquer all their difficulties and keep a foothold there for six months. He sounded disappointed when talking about how they had to end their short migration journey because of one team member's unexpected pregnancy. Nevertheless, Wang was still hopeful about the future opportunities of migrating. He mentioned to me that his web name was "artist that roams all over the world", since that was the aspiration he had for himself. He also seemed impressed when he learned that I was studying in the UK. He once said to me during a casual chat, "You know, I kind of admire you. As a Hani, you managed to travel so far to the UK. That's something!" It is clear that for Wang, and many other young informants like him, mobility was seen as a desirable experience, as it was seen as a part of their self-making project to be modern citizens.

Indeed, Wang thinks all of his migration experiences make him more confident and mature, and even set him apart from his less mobile peers. There were two other Lahu girls in Tea Park – Yi and Qin. They were both very young – aged 17 and 18 – and they came from a village adjacent to

Wang's. It was their first migration experience. They learned from Wang that Tea Park was hiring new performers, so they went to work there. Yi and Qin were always together wherever they went. They usually talked to each other in Lahu, and they often seemed shy and quiet in front of other people (especially during occasions when they had to speak in the local dialect, which is more similar to Mandarin than Lahu).

When I told Wang that I would like to interview Yi and Qin as well, Wang seemed doubtful that I could successfully get them to talk with me. He even seemed a bit apologetic for the shyness and quietness of his fellow Lahu friends:

> 'They are different from me. I've been to a lot of places, and have seen the world for myself [*jianshimian*], so I'm very confident. See how I can talk with you so confidently and fluently? I doubt that they could [referring to Yi and Qin]. Once during a meeting, the manager asked them something, they just sat there and said nothing ... That was embarrassing!' (Wang, 21 years old, male, Lahu, Tea Park)

From Wang's words, it was clear that he thought it was his previous migration experience that set him apart from his peers, unlike the silent Lahu girls who were too shy to talk to strangers. Wang attributed this to his extensive migration adventures, which exposed him to different experiences – as the *jianshimian* (out to see the world) discourse suggests. These experiences also equipped him with certain qualities and skills, such as being able to talk confidently and articulately.

Being embarrassed by his Lahu counterparts also suggested a sense of shame related to the idea that ethnic minorities are dull, shy, and silent, and consequently do not know how to conduct themselves properly during social occasions. Part of what Wang aspires to achieve by migrating is to avoid such shame by exposing himself to new experiences and consequently becoming a more confident person. From Wang's case, we can see the ways that desire often works through the engendering of certain emotions, and that people respond to this desire by trying to invoke, manage, or avoid certain emotions, such as the shame that relates to unfulfilled desires.

It can also be informative to pay attention to how informants talk about their less mobile counterparts, as it can reveal what mobility means to them. I sometimes heard young informants talk about friends who had stayed at home and did not move. Judging from the ways that they talked about these people, it seemed almost immoral for a young person to stay immobile unless they had a legitimate reason – for example, taking care of sick family member or helping with house building at home. Otherwise, staying immobile is linked with a lack of effort toward self-improvement. As Yi (2011) points out, in certain contexts, those who embrace mobility in order to improve their *suzhi* and modern values are regarded as morally superior to those who stay immobile. Such a mentality is shaped by the fact that the urban is associated with the modern while the rural and the ethnic is associated with backwardness (see also Mao et al, forthcoming).

The association between modernity and mobility in Wang's thinking is not unique. In fact, one of the ways that the state exercises its cultural authority around mobility is to turn rural migrants into modern citizens by various disciplinary discourses and practices (Nyíri, 2010). *Suzhi* discourse is definitely among them. This is the expectation that migrants should improve their *suzhi* through migration, as migration is regarded as an inexpensive substitute for education (Murphy, 2002: 45). In general, migration becomes a major way for migrants like Wang to embrace the modern self. Borrowing Rofel's (2007) terminology, becoming a mobile, modern person is a part of their 'desiring selves'. That is, it is important to understand the yearning and longing to be modern if we want to understand what mobility means to migrants.

As is also evident in Wang's case, the meaning of mobility and the desire to be modern should also be understood in relation to the connotations attached to ethnic minorities in China. Modernization has always been a central part of China's nation-building project, but not all people are equally incorporated into the modernization process. In a study of overseas Chinese and ethnic minority people in China, Barabantseva (2010) convincingly argued that the two groups are regarded as opposing embodiments of China's modernization process, with the former being the representation of modern values and the latter being associated with 'backwardness, poverty, and traditional values' (Barabantseva, 2010: 16). She uses the term 'localization' to show how ethnic minority people are not equally incorporated in the modernization project, as they become 'bearers of ethnic minority identity who represent territorial and cultural spaces assigned to them by the state' (Barabantseva, 2010: 144). Therefore, while mobile overseas Chinese people represent modernization, ethnic minorities are 'attached to a particular locality', both physically and culturally (Barabantseva, 2010: 144). In that sense, it is understandable that ethnic minority migrants are using mobility as a way to reject localization and embrace the modern self.

Particular tensions exist between ethnic performers who perform the 'localized' ethnic culture and tourists who, through tourism and cultural consumption, are on the way to becoming modern and patriotic citizens (Nyíri, 2010). As described in the previous chapter, a major part of the performers' work is to portray the imagined ethnic minority, which places them on the opposite end of modernization. As ethnic culture in China is celebrated as if the evolution of the ethnic minorities has been frozen in time, ethnic performers become the cultural bearers of this 'stillness' and 'locality'. That is part of the reason that mobility is used as a way to reject the localized self and to embrace the modern self. This point will be discussed more thoroughly in the next chapter, which concerns encountering ethnic borders.

When modernity and rurality/ethnicity become two ends of the spectrum, informants work on the project of self by embracing mobility in order to become modern. However, ironically, it is after migration that performers are reminded daily about their outsider status, rurality, and low *suzhi*. As a result, they constantly encounter the rural–urban bordering process during and while off work. At the same time, their border struggles further contribute to the hegemonic meaning of the rural–urban divide, as the divide remains something difficult to challenge. In a way, performers' encounters also show how the cultural authority of the state (Nyíri, 2010), which largely shapes the meaning of rural and urban, is experienced by people in personal, emotional, and intimate ways.

Encountering rural–urban borders in everyday work and lives

Rural–urban borders are experienced during informants' everyday work lives. For example, the need to discipline workers and raise their *suzhi* seems to be obvious to the managers in Tea Park, as most workers there are recruited from adjacent villages. The managers of Tea Park often comment on how the park is a good tourist resource, but one that seems to be compromised by the low *suzhi* of the workers. Therefore, when I was doing fieldwork in Tea Park, there was a ritual every morning whereby two office staff would teach workers polite manners to use when greeting the tourists. Firstly, the workers' use of Mandarin was corrected if they spoke with a strong accent. There was training targeting workers' body language when they greeted the guests; for example, they were taught to always allow the tourists to pass first, and at the same time to say 'after you'. Most of the workers found these short training sessions ridiculous. Sometimes they laughed and commented on the uselessness of the training, but these were mandatory meetings which every worker had to attend every morning.

Workers' bodies and accents were under scrutiny as well. When I worked with informants in Waterfall Restaurant, sometimes I did get comments about my bodily appearance. Once, while I was sweeping the floor, a table of guests summoned me in front of them – it seemed that they had been observing me from a distance for a while. One of them asked: "You are not an ethnic minority person from a local area, right?" As I was wondering why such a question was asked, another of them added: "Because your skin tone is fairer than the others." Realizing what the guests meant, I tried to answer ambiguously since it is important to leave guests with the impression that we are all authentic ethnic minority people. I said that my skin tone was lighter because I had just come back from another province. The guests let me go once their curiosity was satisfied. There was also another time when guests commented on how it was weird to see ethnic minority people wearing glasses, which I do. Wearing glasses is a symbol embodying high cultural quality, which is also related to having high *suzhi*. This does not fit with guests' imaginary of what ethnic minority people should look like. These little incidents all show the embodied element of ethnicity.

Along with bodily appearance, informants' accents were also under scrutiny. In most cases, accent was the element that set rural people apart from their urban counterparts. Once I overheard a conversation between the restaurant owner, Ms Yang, and a 7-year-old girl named Jiajia, who was the daughter of a migrant performer working in the restaurant. Although born and raised in Green City, Jiajia spoke the local dialect with a rural accent, just like her mother. Ms Yang half-jokingly said to her: "Jiajia, you should stop speaking like your mom. You will be looked down upon by other people if you continue speaking with a rural accent." Jiajia did not respond, and the conversation soon shifted to other topics among the group of people who were present. Ms Yang was not groundless when she suggested Jiajia's rural accent could incur discrimination. In fact, accent as a 'particular expression of classed embodiment' does relate to different kinds of emotions, such as shame (Loveday, 2016: 1146). The ways that shame was engendered in relation to accent also revealed the embodied dimension of *suzhi*, which Sun (2009: 619) terms as 'corporeal evidence': 'the complexion, hairstyle, accent, speech, body language, and, by extension, clothes of the mobile body'. The low *suzhi* associated with migrant bodies also constitutes their 'out-of-placeness' (Sun, 2009: 632). Here, the irony emerges, as performers seek to use migration to become modern (as shown in the previous section) while at the same time being deemed out of place, and therefore lacking value and quality.

As a way of resistance, informants sometimes seek to re-frame the meaning of 'the rural'. During their casual chats, or during interviews with me, some of the informants would comment upon how urban life was no longer so desirable because of problems such as pollution and food security risks. However, rural–urban encounters at work still continue to shape their sense of entitlement, as well as what kind of people they aspire to become. When the right to access respect and full citizenship is still largely attached to urban middle-class people, and when hegemonic discourses about modern citizens and the good life still exist, 'aspirational urbanism' becomes the most common response (Otis, 2011). That is, migrant workers' response to their marginal position by dressing up like, and longing to become, urbanites has actually become part of many informants' desirable personhood, as well as a way of trying to add more value to themselves. One of the ways informants do that is through after-work entertainment, which was discussed in the previous chapter. Another important way for informants to add value to themselves as migrant performers is to foster talents and cultivate ethnic selves. This requires them to embrace the 'ethnic scripts' that are promoted by the market and the state. This will be discussed in the next chapter concerning performers' intimate experiences of ethnic borders.

Conclusion

In this chapter, I have discussed how informants constantly negotiate the borders along the rural and the urban, and how they experience such border-crossing intimately and emotionally.

Hukou is one of the major mechanisms that has constructed and sustained the long-standing rural–urban divide in China. While it is widely acknowledged that not having an urban *hukou* makes migrants' lives difficult in the cities, it might be surprising and puzzling to find that many migrants are not willing to transfer their *hukou* to the cities, even if they are entitled to do so in some small- and medium-sized cities such as Green City. Existing research suggests that the declining value of urban *hukou* and the rising value of rural *hukou* could explain this '*hukou* puzzle'. However, I argue that this theory largely neglects the role of emotions in this process, and implies that migrants have access to all the information they need to make rational decisions. In reality, migrants are exploring an opaque and fast-changing migration regime, which can be even more confusing for 'outsiders' without local connections.

After exploring the different kinds of emotions that are engendered through migrants' encounters with or imaginaries of *hukou* policy, the concept of 'emotional regime' was used to understand these emotions in relation to its social and historical context, that is, the neoliberal governance in China. To be more specific, in line with the state's promotion of 'happiness' and 'positive energy', as well as the ideology of 'the China Dream', migrants use emotional management to re-frame their negative emotions as positive ones. That is, instead of showing their discontent about the unequal migration regime of *hukou*, they re-frame it as part of their own individual responsibility to achieve success and thus gain entitlement to full citizenship in the city.

Using intimacy as a lens to explore informants' emotional experiences of *hukou* points to the fact that *hukou* is not just to do with the state, but has become a daily practice of valuing the rural and the urban, and the different personhoods associated with them. Therefore, migrants' experiences of *hukou* cannot be merely captured by referenced to its administrative dimension, as it is also deeply embedded in personal, everyday experiences.

It also needs to be made clear that I am not arguing that informants are making these decisions purely based on emotions, nor are they rationally considering the pros and cons. Rather, I am suggesting that emotions colour these processes and must be taken into account if we want to get a better understanding of the *hukou* puzzle. Additionally, these emotions can be informative in revealing some aspects of the operation of *hukou* as a form of formal citizenship – for example, how it becomes a form of reward in China, and how it assumes sedentarism as the norm while in a sense problematizing mobility. These emotions are better understood in relation to the broader social contexts that situate them, as shown in the discussion of emotional regime.

On the one hand, the rural–urban borders are constructed and manifested through concrete policies and rules such as *hukou*. On the other hand, borders are also sustained through the different meanings attached to the rural and the urban, while the state's cultural authority plays an important role in this construction. Therefore, intimacy as a lens also reveals how border struggles over the rural–urban divide has a profound impact on migrant performers' sense of self as they embrace mobility to achieve modern selves. However, the fact that they have to dress up like ethnic minorities at work also poses the contradiction between the desired modern, urban self, and the undesired rural, ethnic, backward self at work. How do migrant performers struggle with such contradictions? And what kinds of impact do such border struggles have on their emotions, sense of self, and relationships? It is difficult to fully understand the bordering process along the rural–urban divide without thinking about the issue of ethnicity and gender. Therefore, the following chapters will continue this exploration by focusing on the dimensions of ethnicity and gender.

Note

Parts of this chapter were previously published as: Mao, J. (2023) Bringing emotional reflexivity and emotional regime to understanding 'the hukou puzzle' in contemporary China, *Emotions and Society*, Bristol University Press. Retrieved 17 November 2023, from https://doi.org/10.1332/263169021 X16731871958851 (reproduced with permission).

4

Encountering Ethnicity

Introduction

This chapter continues to explore migrant performers' intimate struggle over borders. Just like the rural–urban divide, ethnicity is a form of border that migrant performers encounter in their migration journey as well as in daily work. By using intimacy as a lens – more specifically by understanding informants' ambivalence over the meaning of ethnicity – a potential new way to understand ethnicity emerges, one which regards ethnicity as something people do rather than who they are. The concept of 'ethnic scripts' emerges as this chapter continues to explore what shapes the ways that people do ethnicity. Further, the ability for borders to produce subjectivity is highlighted as I explore how ethnic scripts are actively incorporated into migrant performers' projects of self. As the intimate lens challenges our existing ways of theorizing ethnicity, it is also crucial to think about encounters with the border as emotional, embodied, and personal. These all point to the importance of addressing the intimate aspect of border struggles.

Encountering ethnicity: ambivalence and practices

Situated in Southwest China, Yunnan is home to 25 officially recognized ethnic minority groups, while Green City is home to 14, with the major groups including Yi, Hani, Lahu, Wa, and Dai. As mentioned before, Green City's multi-ethnic culture has consistently been highlighted by its tourist industry. The meaning of *minzu*, which literally means ethnicity in Chinese, has been contested and remains extensively debated. For example, it is largely debatable whether the meaning of *minzu* is exactly the same as ethnicity in the Western context, since it carries with it certain connotations that are unique in its context (see, for example, Zang, 2015). While *minzu* used to be translated in English as 'nationality', it was later translated as 'ethnicity' by the state. The shift of the term reflects the underlying normative value of the state in different social and political contexts (see Barabantseva, 2008).

Some scholars also insist that there is no completely equivalent term of *minzu* in English, as *minzu* carries a meaning that cannot be fully captured by 'nationality' or 'ethnicity'. This is largely linked with the emergence of the idea of *minzu* since the 1950s.

The CCP (Chinese Communist Party) engaged in the *minzu* classification project in the 1950s, soon after it came to power. Among the 400 groups that filed applications for recognition, only 55 minority *minzu* groups were eventually officially recognized by the CCP (for a detailed exploration of the *minzu* classification project, see Mullaney, 2011). The eventual *minzu* classification was 'the marriage between social scientific and state socialist practice' (Mullaney, 2011: 118). Although it is not unproblematic, the *minzu* classification project has made *minzu* categories institutionalized and formalized, with every citizen's ID card clearly classifying one's *minzu* since the onset of ID card usage in 1984. Before that, *minzu* categories were also marked on other government documents, such as the *hukou* booklet. A child's ethnicity is registered according to his/her parents' ethnicity, and he/she is eligible to file an application to change ethnic registration after reaching adulthood.

One important finding of this book is that individuals' ethnic self-identifications are not always in accordance with their state registered identities. This is not because of the problem with registration; rather, it is the ambivalent feelings people have regarding the meaning of their ethnic identities. Such ambivalence is particularly salient for migrant performers, who constantly encounter ethnicity in their daily work and lives. Before exploring what this ambivalence tells us about ethnicity, I will illustrate how performers encounter ethnicity during work, and how such encounters evoke some sorts of reflexivity in their thinking and feeling about ethnicity.

Encountering ethnicity in daily work

As ethnic performance is increasingly taken up by people who are not ethnic minorities themselves, it seems at first glance that ethnicity is increasingly irrelevant in ethnic performance settings. As one of the performers named Gao said when commenting on the relationship between one's ethnic identity and ethnic performance: "It is no longer important if you are ethnic minority or not. If you put on ethnic minority costumes, you can be an ethnic minority as well." However, when looked at closely, the performance of ethnicity is not as simple as putting on and taking off clothes, and ethnicity has become an issue which is not only relevant for performers during work. Nonetheless, ethnic performance is 'framed by ethnicity', meaning that ethnicity has deeply shaped the performance setting, and therefore shaped the interactions of people in such settings (see Chapter 2). Before guests step into the ethnic performance setting, they already have in mind that they are going to interact with ethnic minority people. The settings of the workplace, as well as the workers' colourful ethnic costumes, continue to constitute ethnic frames. Therefore, ethnicity is something that performers have to constantly encounter in their everyday work lives. I will illustrate this point by telling the story of an informant named Kai.

Kai is a tour guide in Tea Park. Every day before he starts work he has to put on a minority costume, as it is part of the job requirement for all tour guides in Tea Park. Every day, Kai shows tourists around Tea Park, introducing its tea culture tracing back thousands of years, and its relationships to local minority culture – he learned all these scripts from the tour guide manual produced by the local tourist bureau of Green City, although he needs to adjust some of the lines to make them more in line with Tea Park's scenes. Although a Hani himself, Kai has little recognition of this identity – a point that will be explored further. Nevertheless, Kai often gets questions from tourists about his ethnic identity. Seeing him dressed in an ethnic costume, many guests ask him questions such as which ethnic group he belongs to, what the ethnic culture of his ethnic group is, and whether he speaks the ethnic language. Several times, he has even been asked by tourists to sing ethnic songs for them, although that is not part of a tour guide's work.

Here, multiple aspects of labour are involved. Kai has to present his body and manage emotions in a certain way to meet the expectations of ethnic assessment. Body work and emotional labour are involved in his 'doing ethnicity' at work. Furthermore, the multiplication of labour (Mezzadra and Neilson, 2013) also means that people need to do extra work to turn themselves into what is desired for the work. It is more about the potential to 'become' the right person rather than being the right person. The labour required to work on one's self has become one of the many dimensions of the job. Thus, Kai felt the urgent need to know more about ethnic minority culture in general and what his ethnicity means:

> 'After I took this job [as a tour guide], I felt that I really needed to learn more about Hani culture and customs. It is something essential to learn as a tour guide, as you know, tourism in Yunnan is mainly about ethnic minority cultures. That is what tourists want to see when they go to visit Yunnan.' (Kai, 21 years old, male, Tea Park, tour guide)

Kai's comments about the impact of the work highlight how daily encounters with ethnicity at work have engendered his reflexivity towards the meaning of ethnicity. This is a point that has been observed in previous literature about people who engage in ethnic tourism. For example, in exploring the ethnic tourism in Shangri-La, Yunnan Province, Bai (2007: 257) argues that ethnic tourism serves as 'a daily reminder of ethnicity' for people who participate in it, and push people to think more self-consciously and self-reflexively about the meaning of ethnicity. Other research about ethnic tourism similarly points out how engaging in ethnic tourism has motivated people to think about the meaning of being part of ethnic minorities in contemporary China (see, for example, Li, 2003; Walsh, 2005). However, this literature tends to imply that people can move freely between their on-stage self and off-stage self, which means one's 'authentic self' is detachable from the self at work. This viewpoint largely neglects how the need to constantly encounter ethnicity has a more profound impact on the workers, which they cannot simply get rid of by taking off their work costumes and entering non-work spheres of life.

Another point this literature tends to neglect is people's ambivalent feelings of comfort and discomfort with their ethnic identities. This is a point that was constantly remarked upon in my fieldwork. In other words, rather than assuming that a person is ethnic minority according to his/her *minzu* registration, which I would argue is an essentialized way of understanding ethnicity, it is important to recognize that a person's subjective understanding and feelings towards ethnicity should be taken into account.

For instance, in the case of Kai, although he constantly encounters ethnicity at work, he actually has a lot of ambivalence about his own ethnic identity. Sometimes Kai would feel embarrassed when encountering these requests and questions from tourists, since he knows little about Hani culture and customs. Despite being officially registered as a Hani, Kai does not think himself as an authentic Hani person. His parents migrated away from their Hani village when Kai was very young. Growing up in a Han village, Kai felt that he has partly lost the connection with his ethnic origins:

> 'Hani should be an important identity for me. However, I don't feel that I am an authentic Hani. When I get home, my parents sometimes speak Hani, and I don't understand. I don't know what are the major festivals that Hani should celebrate. I don't know … I want to be a real Hani, but I don't think I can. My parents moved too early, I was only four at that time.' (Kai, 21 years old, male, Hani, Tea Park, tour guide)

Kai's ambivalence was shared by other informants who also had doubts about the meaning of their ethnic identities. In fact, one of the surprises for me as a researcher when entering the field was to find that not all ethnic performers considered themselves as 'authentic' ethnic minorities. Some performers are Han, while others are ethnic minority people from different ethnic origins, mostly Yi, Lahu, Wa, and Dai. It is interesting to discover that even people who are officially registered as ethnic minorities, are ethnic minorities by descent, and have ethnic identities clearly marked on their official identity cards have different understandings and emotions regarding their ethnic identities. "I'm not an authentic minority" (*wo bushi zhengzong de shaoshuminzu*) was a sentence that was repeatedly said to me by informants when I asked them about their ethnicity during my fieldwork. For the convenience of theorizing, I call these people 'ascribed minorities', meaning that they feel their ethnic identities are more like something that has been ascribed to them from somewhere else – state recognition, family heritage, and so on – instead of something they really see themselves to be. If their ethnic identifications are not something that they can sit comfortably with, what do such identifications mean to them? More importantly, why do they think that they are not 'authentic' ethnic minorities? These are the questions that I will explore in this chapter.

Ethnicity as 'doing' rather than 'being'

Insights were gained from informants' explanations when they were trying to define who they thought 'authentic' minorities were. This is revealed in two conversations I had with a performer named Mi and a chef named Chen, both of whom thought of themselves as ascribed ethnic minorities.

Mi:	I am Hani because my mother is Hani. But I think I'm Hanified ... [*wo yijing bei Hanhua le*]. Because in fact I am not much different from Han. Even from my mother's generation, they stopped speaking the Hani language. I can't even listen to Hani language and understand it. (Mi, 21 years old, female, Hani, Forest Park)
Researcher:	[Explains research]
Chen:	I think it will be fruitless if you just keep trying to find ethnic minorities here [meaning in Waterfall Restaurant].
Researcher:	Why is that?
Chen:	Many of the ethnic minorities are inauthentic just like me.
Researcher:	I didn't know that you were ethnic minority!
Chen:	I am. I'm Yi. But ... I don't think I am authentic Yi.
Researcher:	Why is that?
Chen:	I am authentic Yi by blood, but I know nothing about Yi. I know nothing about Yi culture at all, and I don't understand Yi language. My ancestors are all Yi though. My grandfathers from both my mother and my father's sides are Yi.
Researcher:	Can they speak or understand Yi?
Chen:	My father probably can understand Yi when other people are speaking, but he cannot speak Yi. But my grandfather's generation, they can both

> understand and speak Yi. (Chen, 32 years old, male, Yi, Waterfall Restaurant)

Mi and Chen's views are echoed by many informants, for whom ethnic identity is not something that can be strictly defined, but is subject to their own definition. Many factors influence how they think about such identities. For example, both of the informants mentioned the roles of language and costume in playing a role and shaping their sense of being ethnic. Some informants also mentioned their parents' migration, which took them further away from the places where ethnic culture is still practised in villagers' everyday lives, such as noted in the story of Kai. Some of them also situate themselves against the backdrop of the 'Hanification' process, which they think is the major reason that their generation, or even the earlier generation, stopped adopting many ethnic practices.

Just like Mi, many informants use 'Hanification' to explain the reasons that they think they are inauthentic. Hanification or Han assimilation means the process through which ethnic minorities become increasingly assimilated to the Han. It means that they increasingly adopt Han practices, such as speaking Mandarin rather than minority languages. It is related to the state's overarching ideology towards ethnic minorities – *ronghe* ideology – which aims to assimilate minorities into the Han, and eventually eliminate their cultural difference (see Ma, 2007; Zang, 2015). The state also uses the 'civilizing project', such as education, with the aim of eliminating the supposed 'backwardness' of ethnic minorities and thereby enabling them to catch up with the Han (Harrell, 1995). Education for many minority children is also intended to turn them into Chinese citizens, compelling them to choose between being Chinese and being ethnic minorities (Yi, 2005). In a sense, these informants' cases suggest that the project of Han assimilation has been successful. The younger generation of ethnic minority people growing up in the contemporary era has lost its close connection with minority culture. As a result, informants often defined the old people who still remained in the villages as authentic and advised me to find them there.

Although Hanification plays a significant role in explaining why some people stopped these ethnic practices and consequently lost their sense of attachment to their ethnic identities, this is not the only explanation. Informants' descriptions also highlighted the important role of *practices* in their sense of being ethnic. For example, both Mi and Chen's answers highlight the importance of practices such as speaking the language, understanding the language, and having certain knowledge about one's own ethnic group. These are all important parts of one's ethnic belonging. Such senses of being ethnic can be determined not only by blood or ancestry, but can also largely depend on practices.

This echoes existing theory which regards ethnicity as practices rather than pre-existing qualities within people. Building on Bourdieu's theory of practice and habitus (Bourdieu, 1977), Bentley (1987) proposes that by viewing ethnicity as practices which are shaped by the habitus building upon shared experiences, this perspective could shed light on the multidimensionality of ethnicity, including people's affective experience of ethnicity in relation to specific contexts. It is important to note that, like all other practices, the practices of ethnicity are not fully based in individuals' free will – practices are forms of habitus-informed doing (Bentley, 1987).

However, there are reasons why Bentley's approach to the practice of ethnicity cannot be directly applied to our understanding of performers' experiences. In performers' cases, as ascribed minorities, even though they have stopped practising ethnicity because of their changing habitus, they still have to perform or to do ethnicity as part of their work as ethnic performers. For example, although Kai stopped practising ethnicity from a young age (the reason that he gave when defining himself as 'inauthentic'), he still needs to do ethnicity at work, so it is something that he has to encounter every day. Rather than habitus, a number of normative cultural expectations have deeply shaped the ways in which he practices ethnicity. Therefore, while recognizing ethnicity as something people do or practice, I find West and Zimmerman's (1987) theory of 'doing gender' more helpful in terms of thinking about ethnicity as something people do rather than who they are.

Instead of regarding gender as a fixed quality that exists within people, the 'doing gender' approach sees gender as something people do. It is an accomplishment based on men and women's constant 'doing' to live up to social norms regarding femininity and masculinity. It is also important to note that to 'do' gender is not always to live up to normative conceptions of femininity or masculinity; it is to engage in behaviour *'at the risk of gender assessment'* (West and Zimmerman, 1987: 136; emphasis in original). In a similar vein, there are existing normative cultural expectations regarding how people should do ethnicity in China – I call these sets of rules and expectations 'ethnic scripts' (see also Mao, 2023a), which will be explored in the next section – and people can be subject to 'ethnic assessment' in the sense that they are expected to do ethnicity in a way that is in accordance with cultural norms. This is particularly salient for ethnic performers who have to encounter ethnicity on a daily basis and whose work takes place in a setting which is 'framed by ethnicity'. Just as it is well recognized that people need to 'do gender' at work (see, for example, Hall, 1993; Mavin and Grandy, 2013), migrant performers are also expected to do ethnicity at work, and ideally, to do it well.

For instance, to do ethnicity at work, Kai firstly has to dress up in ethnic costumes. He has to equip himself with knowledge about ethnic culture in Yunnan, which is mainly provided by the tourism manual. Indeed, the depiction of ethnic minority people is very similar to the textbook version of ethnicity in China, which one can easily find in textbooks for school children (see Chu, 2015). For example, it depicts how ethnic minority people are naturally born with the talents to be good at singing and dancing, or how being hospitable to guests is ingrained in minority people's warm hearts and pure spirits. Such concepts are also similar to the depictions one can find in the advertisements on many of the billboards in Green City, advertising the colourful ethnic cultures that one can experience there as a tourist. In other words, such representations of ethnic minority people are pervasive in the context of Green City, and thereby become things informants have to constantly encounter and negotiate with.

Therefore, during his work as a tour guide, Kai has to be ready to face questions and comments about ethnicity, especially in relation to his own ethnic identity. He also has the obligation to perform ethnicity when required – for example to show some ability in speaking ethnic languages and singing ethnic songs. All these interactions are under the implicit guideline that guests should be convinced that they are interacting with an authentic ethnic minority person who embodies their imagination about ethnic minorities in Yunnan. This all means that Kai is constantly subject to ethnic assessment at work, and hence he is required to do ethnicity well if he is to be a good ethnic tour guide in Tea Park.

To summarize, a shift of perspective from ethnicity as 'being' to ethnicity as 'doing' would better enable us to understand informants' ambivalence towards their ethnic identities. This perspective of doing ethnicity is a refusal to see ethnicity in an essentialized way; it recognizes that while the state's identification of ethnicity is fixed and rigid, individuals' identifications are fluid and constantly under negotiation (Leibold, 2010).

Just as doing gender is deeply shaped by the normative cultural assumptions about what men and women should be like (West and Zimmerman, 1987), it is also important to ask what has guided and shaped performers' doing of ethnicity. What are the normative expectations of performers when they are doing ethnicity at work? Inspired by scripting theory, especially the theory of 'sexual scripts' (Gagnon and Simon, 1973; Simon and Gagnon, 1986), I argue that the concept of ethnic script can be useful in illuminating performers' experiences of doing ethnicity, both within the work setting and off work.

The multi-layered ethnic scripts in contemporary China

In thinking about ethnicity as something we do, it is important to note that such practices do not exist in a vacuum, as they are informed by existing representations, common knowledge, and cultural expectations of ethnicity, which all form the 'ethnic script'.

'Ethnic script' was proposed as a theoretical concept in existing research on migrants (Lerner et al, 2007). Drawing on script theory, the concept of ethnic script was used to describe prescribed normative behaviour according to one's ethnicity – in this case education was regarded as part of the ethnic script for Russian Jewish immigrants in Israel, who heavily draw on the ethnic script to understand who they are and draw ethnic group boundaries (Lerner et al, 2007). Here, Lerner et al (2007) point out the collective meaning of the ethnic script, meaning that it is not only relevant in individual negotiations of ethnic identities, but also relevant in group identity politics.

While Lerner et al's theory is explanatory in theorizing how group boundaries are drawn by referring to ethnic scripts, their use of 'ethnic script' is more like ethnic stereotypes – in this case how Russian Jewish people as an ethnic group always value education. One could reasonably argue that valuing education is more about 'class' among Russian Jewish intellectuals, rather than an issue that is about ethnicity. More empirical and theoretical evidence is required to legitimize the existence of ethnic scripts in this case. Besides, ethnic script is mainly approached as something individuals use to make sense of a new social environment. Less talked about is how ethnic scripts can be influential in shaping people's behaviours. Further, the ethnic script is approached as a singular matter, while in fact there can be multiple scripts existing simultaneously in defining normative cultural assumptions about the meaning of ethnicity.

Therefore, my use of the concept of 'ethnic scripts' departs from Lerner et al's theory on these points, and I will put more emphasis on how China's context shapes the meaning of ethnic scripts. To be more specific, my use of 'scripts' is closer to the 'cultural scenarios' dimension of the script, in which Simon and Gagnon (1986) discuss sexual scripts. 'Cultural scenarios', in their theorization of sexuality, are the 'cultural narratives constructed around sexuality' which are available for individuals to draw on to make sense of sexuality (Jackson and Scott, 2010: 816). Similarly, my definition of ethnic scripts is also the cultural repertoire of ethnicity, which largely informs people's practices and understandings of ethnicity. There is existing literature which implies that individuals in China make sense of their ethnic identity in relation to the state's representations of ethnicity, although they do not use the term 'ethnic scripts', nor do they systematically analyse it. By using the concept of 'ethnic scripts', I aim to make more explicit the ways that existing cultural scenarios shape individuals' understandings and practices of ethnicity. As the meaning of scripts is to tell people ways to act, scripts reveal the connections between representations and everyday lives. How, then, do ethnic scripts shape my informants' ways of doing ethnicity? It is firstly necessary to briefly explore what the cultural repertoires are and what they say about ethnic minority people in general in China's context.

The multi-layered meaning of ethnic scripts will be explained in relation to existing literatures about the discourses and cultural representations of ethnicity in China. Meanwhile, as ethnic scripts clearly shape the ways ethnic performances are designed and presented, I will also use ethnic performance as an example to explain the meaning of ethnic scripts.

The first layer of ethnic scripts is the binary distinction between the Han and ethnic minorities, which is a recurrent theme in the literature about the cultural representation of ethnicity in China. While ethnic minority people are portrayed as 'the Other', the peripheral, and the exotic, such representations reaffirm the Han's position as the norm, the dominant, and even un-ethnic (Gladney, 1994; Harrell, 1995; Schein, 2000; Leibold, 2010). It could be said that it is performers' otherness, or the ability to perform such otherness, that helped them attain their jobs in the first place (Schein, 2006). Hence, in a sense, for ethnic performers, to do ethnicity at work is to keep performing such differences and otherness. Substantial body work and emotion work are involved in portraying minorities as 'the Other' in society.

Secondly, ethnic minority people are also regarded as backward and primitive, and as associated with the past (Harrell, 1995). Such representations of ethnic minorities share a resemblance with discourses about rural people in China, which depict rurality as opposed to modernity (see Chapter 3). Therefore, the *suzhi* (human quality) discourse is also often used to describe ethnic minority people in similar ways as rural people are portrayed. In fact, being ethnic and being rural are closely related. That is also the reason that people often kindly suggested that I look for authentic minority people in the remote mountainous rural areas. This was also partly because ethnic minority people are imagined to be pure and simple, uncontaminated by modern ways of living. In Forest Park, ethnic performance was incorporated into the natural forest setting, with wild animals living in an enclosed area which was also an attraction for tourists. The dances that performers perform on stage also tell stories about the 'past', such as one about how the Wa used to rely on hunting animals for a living before the socialist regime was established. In that dance, female performers wear grass skirts and their male counterparts wear only shorts. With long sticks in their hands, they imitate primitive people who are trying to hunt tigers for a meal. The primitiveness and backwardness of the ethnic minority people that is portrayed through the performance also further produces their otherness and exoticism.

Another important layer of ethnic scripts is the portrayal of minority women as erotic and subject to different sexual standards (Schein, 2000; Walsh, 2005). This is particularly true for minority women in Southwest China. For example, for the Mosuo in Yunnan, the popular perception of minority women as being sexually promiscuous and available has been utilized by the market to promote ethnic tourism (Walsh, 2005). Before guests set foot in the tourist attraction, they already expect to experience the erotic culture of Mosuo; this has put a lot of pressure on women from the local area, regardless of whether or not they participate in the tourism industry. Local gender relations have been challenged as well (Walsh, 2001). In this research, such gendered and sexualized ethnic scripts shaped the performance sites in various ways, including how female performers are expected to drink cross-cupped wine and to sit on guests' laps. The gendered nature of ethnic scripts will be discussed in more detail in the next chapter.

There are certainly other aspects of ethnic scripts which cannot be summarized in an exhaustive manner here. Just as sexual scripts are multidimensional and constantly changing, ethnic scripts also never remain static and unchanged. It is also crucial to point out how ethnic scripts are clearly guided and shaped by the *ronghe* ideology which aims to eventually assimilate ethnic minorities and promote China as a unified nation with colourful ethnic cultures (Ma, 2007; Zang, 2015). The seemingly paradoxical effort to preserve ethnic cultures and eventually achieve assimilation are not necessarily in contradiction with each other, since states can achieve 'a Han-centric vision of Chinese modernisation' (McCarthy, 2011: 10) by promoting ethnic cultures in state-promoted ways.

In China's context, ethnic scripts are heavily promoted by the state – this leads to the differential judgment of ethnic practices as well. Some ethnic practices are deemed to be good, and are thus distinguished for promotion and protection. Other practices, meanwhile, are regarded as bad, feudal, and superstitious, and it is deemed necessary to eliminate them (see, for example, McCarthy, 2011; Zang, 2015). There are also other ethnic practices that are deemed dangerous, as they are associated with national separatism. For example, many ethnic groups in China have religious backgrounds, and some of their religious practices, especially those in relation to cross-border religious practices, are deemed as dangerous and a potential risk to national unity (see also Rippa, 2020). When I was doing my fieldwork in Green City, I followed one of my informants to her home village at the time of the Spring Festival. It was a Lahu village with Christian traditions. I observed a scene wherein a village official was complaining about how the local priest was secretly distributing religious materials from Myanmar, the border of which is just a few miles away from this village. Since there is a group of Lahu in Myanmar, with whom the Lahu people who live near the border in Yunnan may have more cultural proximity than with the Han, their interactions were under close surveillance by the local government. When a conversation I was having with another local official shifted to the topic of 'religion', he suddenly refused to continue the conversation with me. Being aware that I was studying at a foreign university, this local official refused to discuss 'sensitive' topics with me. However, from his responses, it is clear that certain ethnic practices are not deemed to be as harmless as others.

Another issue that needs to be considered is whether there is an ethnic script for each distinct group. Without denying that each minority group might have their own distinct script, I would argue that ethnic scripts provide an overwhelmingly hegemonic depiction of ethnic minorities in general in China. Under such a homogeneous normative representation, the distinct ethnic group disappears and is replaced by the umbrella term 'ethnic minorities' (*shaoshu minzu*). This means that ethnic minority groups are largely treated as homogeneous, although they have different cultures and traditions.

While giving a homogeneous representation of ethnic minorities, it is important to point out that there are multiple ethnic scripts, and these ethnic scripts do not always give clear and coherent messages about ethnicity in China. For example, there are ethnic scripts which are clearly endorsed by the state (for example, 'Eliminate poverty, and not let one *minzu* brother or sister left behind'), and others which are promoted by the market to gain profits (for example, 'Be ready to be welcomed by our most hospitable and pure ethnic minority people'). More often than not, these different dimensions of ethnic scripts coexist, and it is difficult to distinguish which one is the government's version or the market version. Therefore, ethnic scripts originate from different sites, while the local variants which are from different sources add other layers to them. In other words, ethnic scripts are multi-layered, sometimes may conflict with each other, and can be mobilized in different contexts in different ways.

It is also important to point out that the ethnic scripts that are discussed in this chapter mainly apply to ethnic minorities in Southwest China, and Yunnan Province in particular. I have mentioned how Yunnan often seems to be a peaceful region relatively low in *minzu* conflicts or controversies. Therefore, the ethnic scripts that are described here may not apply to other contexts such as Xinjiang or Tibet. While the idea of ethnic scripts may be employed in different contexts, it is always important to recognize the local dimension of ethnic scripts, and to understand them in contextualized ways.

More importantly, although ethnic scripts seem to exist at the macro level, as they are more about the broader social and cultural context, it is crucial to explore how they work through individuals in the most micro and intimate ways. As I seek to show in the following theorization, migrant performers' emotions and projects of self are heavily informed by existing ethnic scripts.

Cultivating the ethnic self: emotion, personhood, and ethnic scripts

The emotional politics of ethnicity
How do ethnic scripts as a concept help us to think about migrant performers' intimate negotiations over the border of ethnicity? I argue in this section

that ethnic scripts work in a similar way to 'feeling rules', which not only shape the ways that performers do emotion work within work settings, but also shape their emotional negotiations over being ethnic minorities in contemporary China.

At work, performers are expected to do 'emotion work' in relation to the ethnic scripts. Both 'emotion work' and 'emotional labour' point to the need for people to manage their emotions, with the latter being more about the emotion work people do for paid work (Hochschild, 1979). Here, I choose to put 'emotion work' at the centre of the inquiry instead of 'emotional labour'. This is because 'emotional labour' implies a dualism of the public and the private, as well as paid and unpaid work, which this book is trying to challenge, as the boundary between work and the personal becomes blurred. While 'emotion work' was used to refer to how people manage emotions in private (Hochschild, 1979), the work that performers undertake crosses private/public boundaries. Moreover, it is difficult to distinguish the emotion work that people do as ethnic minorities with the part that they do as ethnic performers.

It is acknowledged that the ways that people do emotion work are deeply shaped by feeling rules, which are a set of social and cultural norms governing how people should feel in a certain context (Hochschild, 1983). Feeling rules, as a form of social norm, do not exist alone. This means that they coexist with other social norms in society, such as norms about gender, ethnicity, class, and so on. While the gendered nature of feeling rules is well acknowledged by existing work (see, for example, Lupton, 1998), little research touches on the issue of the racialized or ethnicized aspects of feeling rules.

It is only recently that researchers have started to challenge the racial silence in research about emotions and feeling rules. Kang's (2003) work tries to bridge the gap by focusing on how the different work contexts shaped by varying intersections of race, gender, and class require workers to perform emotional labour and bodily services differently in nail salons (Kang, 2003). Outside of the service work setting, Wingfield's work (2010) points to the ways that workplace feeling rules are racialized in the US context, in that people from different racial groups are subject to different feeling rules. For example, black men are supposed to avoid showing their anger, since they are trying to avoid being racially stereotyped as 'angry black men', whereas black female workers have more space to show their anger since they are not subject to the same feeling rules that apply to white female workers that require them to be feminine and docile. Hence, the intersection of gender and race influences the feeling rules of the workplace, and therefore shapes how people should feel, or in what ways they should express or suppress their emotions (Wingfield, 2010). Such research points to the importance of challenging the racial silence in the study of feeling rules and emotion work.

My exploration of the emotional politics of ethnicity will also start from 'work'. At work, ethnic performers are subject to feeling rules which largely intersect with ethnic scripts. According to the ethnic scripts at play here, ethnic minority people are passionate, happy, and welcoming to guests. One could argue that as service providers, performers are expected to constantly show hospitality to guests, but ethnic scripts add another layer to the emotion work that performers are expected to do. Performers are expected to constantly show their emotions when providing hospitality to guests and when performing in more dramatic ways, and must present themselves as being part of a cheerful and happy ethnic minority. In fact, there is one popular song named Happy Lahu, which expresses the happiness of the Lahu people living a good life under the communist regime compared to the miserable lives that they were living before the communist party 'liberated' them. Although showing happiness seems to be a feeling rule that similarly applies to the Han and ethnic minorities under the socialist regime, it might be dangerous for ethnic minorities to not show their happy faces, as it implies a national separatist orientation. Here, the 'happiness duty' again falls on the shoulders of ethnic performers: they are not only expected to speak about happiness, but also, crucially, not to speak about unhappiness (Ahmed, 2010).

At the same time, the undertaking of the happiness duty makes migrant performers valuable subjects under the commercialization of ethnicity. Many tourists come to ethnic tourism with the expectation of viewing the happy minorities whose happiness is uncontaminated by modern ways of living (see, for example, Harrell, 1995; Walsh and Swain, 2004). Ethnic minority people tend to be portrayed as worry-free and easily contented by limited material conditions. There is a local saying, which is frequently used as part of the script for ethnic performance, that is used to describe the Lahu people: '[Lahu people] sing once they are full, they dance as long as they have drunk enough wine.' It implies that Lahu people do not need to worry about tomorrow. There is also a negative connotation attached to the saying, which suggests that Lahu people are short-sighted and lazy. It is also often used to justify the Lahu's disproportionate vulnerability to poverty. In the ethnic tourism context, sayings like this are often utilized to showcase the exoticism of ethnic minorities who are subject to different feeling rules when compared to the Han.

The emotion work that migrant performers undertake also requires them to endure prejudices against minority people at work. They have to regulate their feelings about potential discrimination and prejudice. The stereotypes and discrimination associated with ethnicity manifest themselves in performers' daily working lives. It usually means that workers have to do extra emotion work to cope with the biases and stereotypes that are projected onto them. As Bao, a young performer in Forest Park, noted:

'Yes, they think because we are dressed in minority costumes, we know nothing about the outside world. Once a tourist, a man, he really looked down upon us. He thinks that we knew nothing, and we hadn't even watched TV before. At that time, Yuan [his colleague] was angry and wanted to argue with him. I said to her, there is no need to be angry. It's only possible the man has a steady salary, and we might earn more than him. Yes, I think in this way.' (Bao, 26 years old, male, Wa, Forest Park)

Bao's account suggests that the intersection of ethnicity and class has shaped performers' daily working lives. In that situation, Bao had to do extra emotion work to regulate his colleague's and his own emotional response to the tourist's discriminatory remarks. It is also important to acknowledge that monetary power has become a way that Bao justifies certain emotion rules for himself and his colleague. Their financial capabilities are used to mitigate their negative feelings towards such discriminatory situations. As the performers in Forest Park are paid quite well compared to other migrant workers – because of the extra income they receive from the additional *bancan* rituals that they undertake during off-work hours – Bao is able to feel some kind of empowerment because of his financial capability. Here, his sense of entitlement to respect is related to economic status. This, in turn, is also deeply shaped by 'hegemonic masculinity', which associates masculinity with monetary power (Choi and Peng, 2016). This kind of sentiment has been shared by many other migrant workers in this research who are trying to earn more money in order to become respectable. This has become another motivator pushing them to work harder, work for longer hours, and work under exploitative conditions. This also is part of the reason that migrant performers are trying to develop the 'enterprising self' (Rose, 1992), and trying to capitalize on ethnicity by working on their projects of self. This will be discussed in the following section.

Ethnic scripts can also be used to understand some informants' ambivalence about whether or not they are authentic minorities. Informants' ambivalence towards their ethnic identities may also reflect how ethnicity is only valued in the work setting, in which it can become a valuable asset, but not outside of work. I have mentioned how migrant performers change their ethnic costumes right away after work, and they spend a lot of money on dressing in a fashionable and 'modern' way. This may suggest their wish to 'pass' as Han in their everyday lives.

Meanwhile, while people may draw heavily on existing ethnic scripts to make sense of their ethnicity, there could be a large gap between everyday practices of ethnicity and ethnic scripts. It is ironic that sometimes ethnic scripts override people's everyday experiences of ethnicity and become the 'authentic' ones. I was initially surprised when I found that performers are not very critical of the existing scripts of ethnicity, most of which are essentialized ways of describing ethnic minority people. For example, there were some introductory lines that the host had to say before each performance started, which were mostly about the characteristics of certain minority groups, and these were then reflected in the songs or dances that followed. Such introductory lines are very similar to the wording used in textbooks to introduce ethnic minorities in China, which provide an essentialized understanding of ethnic minority people. According to such depictions, for example, the Wa people are regarded as bold and unrestrained, while Dai people are thought to be gentle and attentive. I was surprised that most informants agree with such scripts, and refer to them when they are talking about their understandings of ethnic groups. However, later, I realized that this shows exactly the ways that ethnic scripts work. In other words, this shows how powerful the impact of ethnic scripts is, with people starting to define ethnicity in relation to what has been prescribed rather than their real-life experiences.

Besides, ethnic scripts as feeling rules are constraining and empowering at the same time. It is also true that sometimes performers are trying to challenge existing ethnic scripts in different ways, or they try to use ethnic scripts in a way that is to their advantage. A host named Huang in Forest Park shared his story of trying to speak some simple English words in front of guests to show them that ethnic minority people could be modern as well. By doing that, he is intentionally challenging the ethnic scripts which depict the backwardness of ethnic minorities.

Sometimes performers also refer to ethnic scripts to urge guests' compulsory drinking. I have observed performers saying things like, "If you don't finish the drink, you will risk jeopardizing ethnic unity in China", or "You have to respect our ethnic culture." In this way, performers are able to put a swifter end to the toasting ritual. Otherwise they would spend too much time interacting with guests and urging them to drink. By referring to ethnic scripts, which emphasize ethnic unity in China, performers try to put themselves in a more powerful position when interacting with the guests. Sometimes female performers also refer to ethnic scripts to reframe the meaning of sexualized labour. This will be further discussed in the next chapter.

In summary, ethnic scripts are influential in shaping how individuals feel about their ethnic identities, and the ways that they engage in emotion work in relation to ethnicity. Ethnic scripts are also useful in helping us understand how migrant performers engage in projects of self in various ways.

Cultivating talents and working on the ethnic self

The development of ethnic tourism and the commercialization of ethnicity in Green City make ethnicity a valued asset. Stories have been shared by local and central media about how ethnic individuals achieve success by becoming ethnic performers or actors. Such stories are also popularly shared among performers. There are ethnic villages which manage to achieve 'poverty alleviation' through engaging in ethnic tourism. The ways that economic development is framed in the context of Green City as an ethnic region specifically points to the connection between poverty alleviation, economic development, and the commercialization of ethnicity. In a way, one could argue that promoting one's ethnic self has come to be one of the ethnic scripts in the local context. In other words, learning to be ethnic has been incorporated into individuals' projects of self, as they strive to access ethnicity as a form of resource in order to achieve 'valuable personhood' (Skeggs, 2011).

Returning to Kai's story at the beginning of this chapter, it is interesting that the commercialization of ethnic culture promoted his willingness to know more about his ethnic origins, even though he never thought of himself as an authentic minority before. For him, to 'work on the ethnic self', or to do ethnicity in a certain way, could potentially be rewarded by the market. Such an effort to work on one's ethnic self does not only apply to performers who are ascribed minorities, but is also true for 'authentic' minorities.

During an afternoon break in Tea Park, I was staying with the ethnic performers to observe their work lives, including the 'boring times' when there were no performances or visiting guests. Wei, a Lahu performer, was singing a popular song accompanied by his guitar. After he had finished, we started to have a conversation. Wei said that he thought he needed to use more time to practise ethnic songs, despite the fact that he was actually more interested in popular songs. I asked him the reason, and he said, "Because wherever you go to *dagong*, many places need you to sing ethnic songs. When the audiences see you, they also expect to hear ethnic songs, not others." Thus, being aware that the commercialization of ethnic culture is taking place in Green City, Wei is consciously cultivating his skills and talents as an ethnic performer.

Growing up in a Lahu village, Wei thinks of himself as an authentic Lahu. However, later in the interview, Wei told me that he never knew how to sing ethnic songs or play guitar before he came to work in Tea Park in 2015. In his own words, he had never "touched a guitar before". People in the village do sing Lahu songs during important rituals such as church gatherings and the Spring Festival celebration. However, these songs are drastically different from the songs that are performed during ethnic performances. Also, working in Tea Park, Wei had to learn songs and dances from other ethnic groups as well. Nevertheless, his friend's successful story of finding a job as an ethnic performer inspired him, and he decided to give it a go.[1] He started to practise guitar at home, and learnt some ethnic songs by himself. This training continued after he got the job in Tea Park.

It is ironic that even though Wei is an 'authentic' Lahu, who grew up in a Lahu village and practises ethnicity in his daily life, he still needs to learn to be ethnic in a certain way that is demanded by the market. Here again, somehow, what ethnic scripts depict as 'authentic' overrides Wei's own experiences and becomes the 'authentic' that is recognized by the market and the state. Practising guitar and singing are not just about skills, but also about learning to embrace the ethnic self that will be desired by the market. While there are limited resources that ethnic minority people like Wei can access – not through education or social capital – ethnicity becomes an available resource one can draw upon to achieve a 'valuable personhood'. In other words, the commercialization of ethnicity, and the use of ethnicity as a means to achieve something, has been incorporated in performers' projects of the self. Here, the commodity frontier (Hochschild, 2003a) does not only extend from the sphere of work to the sphere of home, but also extends to the subjective sphere, and shapes a person's subjectivity and sense of self. Therefore, there is a necessity for individuals to work on themselves to attain the image that is desired by the market. In another interview, Wei detailed his reason for choosing ethnic performance as work:

Wei: I've been looking for a job since I came back from *Guangzhou* [working in the factory]. I want to look for a job that has some space for advancement.

Researcher: What do you mean?

Wei: If it is just about earning money, I might as well go back to *Guangzhou* to continue working in that factory. I wish to have some space for self-development and also career advancement …. After giving it a lot of thought, I decided that for a person like me, the best choice is … to sing these ethnic songs. To choose this road is my best choice.

Researcher: Why is that?

Wei: Because as people like us …. Firstly, you don't have good educational qualifications. In that case it's only manual labour you can do. Even if you can learn some skills from doing the labour, it's still very difficult for you to progress. If you choose to become a performer, and choose to sing ethnic songs … you don't need much cultural knowledge. As long as you are willing to learn. That's why I chose this road. (Wei, 26 years old, male, Lahu, Tea Park)

Even though it means that he will be constantly working on the skills and self images that fit the market's desire to see 'authentic' ethnic minority performers, in comparison to the tiring work in the factories, where there are few career development opportunities, ethnic performance seems like a good career choice for Wei. He seems to be very aware of the importance of developing oneself, as he repeated the term 'develop' (*fazhan*) several times in the interview. Working on the ethnic self does not only provide him with opportunities to find work as an ethnic performer, it also affords him chances of progression and self-development.

Many other informants – mostly men – also talked about 'self-development' quite a lot in their interviews. It is noteworthy that they often associated one's own self-development with local economic development and the promotion of ethnic cultures. The following is an example of how very aware of the market logic and the logic of development informants are, and how they try to situate themselves in that framework of development and fostering talent.

Lang:	Have you heard about XX's [a village famous for ethnic tourism] slogan about their people 'once they know how to talk, they naturally know how to sing; once they can walk, they can dance'?
Researcher:	Yes I've heard. What do you think about that?
Lang:	These are just bullshitting [*huyou*], of course. They tell the visitors that, so they will buy tea from there. So the people's life will improve. If you don't say such bullshit, who will come to tour the place and buy stuff right? See how all the tourist groups keep coming to their village? You have to learn how to bullshit. A person needs to constantly learn new stuff, or he/she will be left behind. (Lang, 27 years old, male, Lahu, Forest Park)

Working on the ethnic self does not only involve practising skills as performers, but also involves knowing how to present ethnic cultures in a certain way that is appealing to outsiders. It is also to constantly work on one's self in accordance with the existing ethnic scripts, especially those endorsed by the state and the market. Here, working on the ethnic self has been actively incorporated into each performer's 'enterprising self', which means that contemporary individuals manage their selves as if they are projects which need to be constantly worked on in various ways (Rose, 1992). Furthermore, the fear of being 'left behind' is shared by informants other than Lang. Many of them internalize the ethnic scripts which depict ethnic minorities as backward and primitive, and consequently feel an urgent need to improve and develop themselves in order to not be left behind.

Such senses of constant self-development and self-improvement are also related to mobility. In the previous chapter, I mentioned the story of Wang, who used to be a performer in Tea Park, and later was discovered by a businessman who invited him to perform in his restaurant in Shanghai. Wang always takes pride in that experience of travelling and experiencing the outside world. He is also convinced that the opportunity of such mobility is a reward for his efforts to work on his ethnic self. Just like Wei, Wang also learned guitar starting from a zero background in order to get a job in Green City as a performer. Although he returned to Green City after working in Shanghai for six months, Wang is convinced that he will eventually get to a greater stage in his career as long as he keeps practising performance skills and keeps working on his ethnic self.

Wang's migration story also shows how the ability to perform the 'localized' and traditional version of ethnic culture affords him a certain status which enables him to be mobile. He told me about how their performance at the ethnic styled restaurant in Shanghai was greatly appreciated by audiences who sought out a taste of 'authentic' ethnic culture. In a study of musicians in Guinea, West Africa, Gaudette (2013) uses the example of 'the Jembefola's path' to describe how African drummers convert their 'traditional' music and culture into physical mobility to the Western world, whereby some of them manage to gain social mobility (Gaudette, 2013). Through African drummers' stories, we can get a glimpse of unequal power relations on a global scale. In a sense, Wang's migration story to Shanghai also resembles the African drummers' story in that mobility was gained on the basis of utilizing traditional cultures which were thought to remain immobile. While the link of traditional ethnic culture with immobility and localized characteristics has been pointed out in previous theorizations in the Chinese context (see, for example, Barabantseva, 2010), individuals like Wang actively employ mobility to embrace modern and potentially cosmopolitan selves.

From Wei's, Lang's, and Wang's stories, we can see how migrant performers like them feel the need to constantly foster skills and develop themselves – be that performance skills, social skills or mobility – or risk being left behind and miss opportunities to progress. In the context of the commercialization of ethnic culture, the instrumentalization of ethnicity is becoming a valued asset, and is being actively incorporated into the performers' projects of self. However, to work on the ethnic self, in a way, is also to maintain the image of primitiveness and backwardness. It is to do ethnicity in a way that emphasizes one's difference and otherness. In this way, performers also actively participate in the production and reproduction of ethnic scripts on a broader level. Meanwhile, it is also important to note that it is mostly men who tend to work on their ethnicized selves and foster their talents, because they are less likely to be sexualized when undertaking performance work.

However, performers' efforts to develop themselves and cultivate skills do not necessarily make them more respectable. The more they try to maintain and develop their ethnic selves, the more they are subject to prejudice and viewed as stereotypes. Ethnicity as an asset is valuable in certain ways, but not in others. Take the embodiment aspect of ethnicity for example: it is clear that ethnicized bodies are becoming desirable in the context of the commodification of ethnicity. Although Han people can also 'pass' as ethnic performers, business owners believe that ethnic minority people, or at least rural people, may embody the bodily characteristics that make such performances seem more authentic. The team leader from Tea Park once shared with me his story of driving to a remote Lahu village to recruit "the right bodies". He insisted that Han people could not add the "flavour" that was desirable in the performance. He ended up bringing five young women and men from that village to work in Tea Park. The newly recruited performers did not know how to sing or dance, so the team leader needed to train them from the beginning. Nevertheless, he considered this recruitment trip, as well as the intensive training, a worthy investment, as it would be converted into the park's revenue later. In this sense, the commodification of ethnicity not only enables ethnicized bodies to become assets with market values, it also enables mobility – as shown through Wang's story. The embodied element has also been incorporated into informants' projects of self. One female performer named Xiaomei once said to me: "There was one point when I thought about dying my hair brown. But later I dropped this idea because I realized that it was important to retain the authentic image of an ethnic minority (*baochi yuanzhiyuanwei*)." This shows how performers actively avoid doing certain 'modernizing' body work in order to maintain their 'authentic' bodies.

However, desirable ethnicized bodies are at the same time the embodiment of low *suzhi*. During a chat I once had with one of the managers of Tea Park, he reacted with shock at my willingness to live in the ethnic performers' dormitory. He said: "Are you sure you want to do that? Their dormitory stinks!" His reaction reflected how ethnic migrants' bodies were imagined in a way that embodied a lack of good hygiene practices, a view which is common in *suzhi* discourses concerning rural and ethnic minority people. Indeed, the identification of ethnic Others having an (unpleasant) smell is a typical form of distinction and ethnic othering, and this is not just restricted to the context of China (see, for example, Charsley and Bolognani, 2017). My later visits to the dormitory proved the manager's impression untrue. It is also ironic to note that having the skills to perform ethnic songs and dances is not regarded as part of the *suzhi*.

Another way that performers try to earn respect is through the reframing of the meaning of ethnic performance:

> 'Many city people are very ignorant about ethnic cultures. Once a group of tourists from other provinces came – all looked well educated – but referred to us as "Ah Wa" rather than "Wa". They never even knew the proper name of our ethnic group! ... I had to tell

them the right name and some basic knowledge about us Wa.' (Xia, 18 years old, female, Wa, Forest Park)

'I like it pretty well [being an ethnic performer]. I think it's a good thing to promote our own ethnic culture [*xuanchuan minzu wenhua*] …. It is even good for our next generation's development if you think about it in a long-term way. It's a beneficial thing for all of us if we succeed in promoting ethnic culture.' (Ai, 23 years old, male, Wa, Forest Park)

By reframing the meaning of ethnic performance as a way to educate urban people who are ignorant about ethnic culture, Xia seeks to attach positive meanings to ethnic performance work, and also to address the power relations between performers and guests differently.

'Promoting ethnic culture' is a narrative that is often used by different actors to justify the meaning of ethnic performance. In a study about ethnic minorities in Yunnan, McCarthy (2011) points out that states are actually promoting multiculturalism to some extent, although it is under certain conditions and with the aim of developing local economies (McCarthy, 2011). In that sense, 'promoting ethnic culture' accords with both state and market interests. It is also interesting to see how performers themselves use this narrative in order to address the importance and meaningfulness of their work. Indeed, Ai mobilizes the discourse that embodies mainstream values in order to depict one's self and work as less marginalized. It is a way for informants to try to 'attach dominant symbolic value to themselves' (Skeggs, 2011: 503)

Also, by embracing the discourse of 'promoting ethnic culture', informants try to include themselves in the state-building project – showcasing China as a multinational unified country. In research about the career development prospects of young professionals, Lisa Hoffman proposes 'patriotic professionalism' to describe how young people are 'wedding individual career development with China's future prosperity' (Hoffman, 2010: 17). Similarly, some informants in this research are also seeking to combine their career advancement with the promotion of ethnic culture and the promotion of China as a unified, multi-ethnic country.

When ethnicity becomes a valuable asset, it is incorporated into the informants' projects of self as a way to achieve valuable personhood. Through working on the ethnic self in a way that fits the ethnic scripts desired by the state and market, informants achieve job opportunities, mobility, and chances of self-development. They closely align their 'enterprising self' with official rhetoric, such as promoting ethnic cultures, boosting local economic development, and so on. Through framing ethnic performance in such ways, they try to incorporate themselves into 'dominant systems of value' (Skeggs, 2011). This framing is also a way for them to fight against marginalization and otherness, whether as working selves or selves in modern society. However, in order to do that, they have to keep working on their ethnic selves, and also, in a way, to keep their otherness and exoticism in order to capitalize on their ethnicity in the context of commercialization. All these things suggest the potential for ethnic scripts to keep changing, as migrant performers and ethnic minority people themselves are also active actors in the production and reproduction of ethnic scripts.

One may wonder whether there are 'negative' emotions involved in this negotiation, such as resentment and anger, considering how informants are expected to constantly reinforce their otherness. As I have argued in the previous chapter, under the current emotional regime which promotes happiness and emphasizes individual responsibility, informants tend to reframe their 'negative' emotions into 'positive' ones. The same argument also applies here. For example, when Bao briefly mentioned his anger at having to deal with guests' prejudice towards ethnic minority people, he emphasized how he successfully managed that emotion. He did so, again, by emphasizing individual success and the ability to earn money and relating these aspects to his ability to promote the ethnic self in a commercialized way. It may also relate to the fact that gendered feeling rules make it difficult for male informants to express their 'negative' emotions to me as a female researcher.

Hence, gender plays an important role here, as the discourse of hegemonic masculinity does not apply to women. Female performers do tend to more freely express their 'negative' emotions, such as their ambivalence about having to undertake sexualized labour. Therefore, it is difficult to understand performers' encountering of borders along the rural–urban divide and ethnicity without thinking about how such encounters are also gendered. I will explore this in more detail in the next chapter.

Conclusion

Ethnic performance is a site of encounter, in which migrant performers have to constantly deal with the issue of ethnicity. This does not only mean how they need to closely interact with the mostly Han customers and give them the impression that they are interacting with 'authentic' ethnic minority people, it also means that symbols and discourses about the right way to be ethnic are pervasive in their daily work lives. However, although ethnic classification is formalized and institutionalized in China, individuals' understandings of ethnicity are fluid and diverse. There are many informants who have ambivalent feelings about whether or not they belong to an 'authentic' ethnic minority or, indeed, what that means in contemporary China.

The lens of intimacy, which takes such ambivalent feelings seriously and asks what we can learn from taking a closer look at these emotions, is useful in revealing a potentially new perspective in understanding ethnicity. Informants' experiences and perspectives challenge the ways that ethnicity is generally viewed as a quality existing within individuals. Therefore, a new perspective is proposed to understand ethnicity as something people do, rather than who they are. This is particularly relevant for migrant performers who have to do ethnicity in their daily work lives and are constantly subject to ethnic assessment. Their doing of ethnicity is assessed in relation to the normative cultural ideas about the 'right way' to be ethnic in China. Meanwhile, their doing of ethnicity is deeply shaped by the existing cultural scenarios of ethnicity in China, which come from various sources – the state, the market, mass media, and so on. I call these cultural scenarios 'ethnic scripts'.

Ethnic scripts in China are heavily state supported, and provide an essentialized and homogeneous understanding of what being ethnic means. According to these scripts, the modern, urban Han are distinguished from the backward, rural minorities. The scripts also eroticize minority women, particularly under the influence of the market, and this impacts on how women do ethnicity in the work context of ethnic performance. In a way, ethnic scripts form feeling rules, which shape how performers do emotion work within and outside of the work context. For example, the emphasis on selling the concept of simple happy minorities unaffected by modern life means that performers need to do extra emotion work above and beyond what they are expected to do as service workers.

They also have to endure prejudices about ethnic minorities from guests during work. Sometimes they do so by drawing on the other scripts which emphasize the promotion of ethnic selves and the value of financial success. This means that they actively incorporate work on the ethnic self into their 'enterprising self'. Because hegemonic ethnic scripts sometimes even override informants' real-life experiences of ethnicity, what ethnic scripts depict comes to be regarded as more authentic than their own lived experiences of ethnicity. However, while some informants may be able to capitalize on doing ethnicity within the work setting, they are very aware that their ethnicity has little value outside of this setting. Therefore, ironically, in order to not to be 'left behind' and be mobile and modern, informants have to do ethnicity in ways that reinforce views of minorities as backward, immobile, and so on. This shows how borders are reinscribed through work on the self.

At the same time, intimacy as a lens also enables us to examine more systematically how work shapes self and emotions, and how the impact of work has deeper implications for the project of self. Migrant performers cultivate their talents and work on their ethnic selves in order to capitalize on their ethnicities and thereby achieve valuable personhood. This is another example of how the work self frames the self. On the other hand, the ways that informants' work on their projects of the self also reinscribe borders.

In this chapter, many theories about ethnicity are borrowed from theories about gender. This is not surprising, as many scholars have already pointed out how the relationship between ethnic minorities and the Han in China is analogous to the relationship of women to men (see, for example, Gladney, 1994; Harrell, 1995; Schein, 2000). This suggests the importance of understanding ethnicity and gender in an intersecting way. An intimately situated way of understanding gender will be explored in the next chapter.

Note

Parts of this chapter were previously published as: Mao, J. (2023) Doing ethnicity: multi-layered ethnic scripts in contemporary China, *The China Quarterly*, 1–15. © The Author(s), 2023. Published by Cambridge University Press on behalf of SOAS University of London (reproduced with permission).

5

Gendering the Border Struggles

In previous chapters, I have shown how migrant performers encounter a series of border struggles in relation to the rural–urban divide and ethnicity. Migrant performers' experiences of encountering these borders through work and migration are emotional and intimate, and often have an impact on their personhood. In this chapter, I seek to show how these border practices and struggles are also inherently gendered. This does not only mean how male performers and female performers experience these borders in different ways, although they certainly do, it also means regarding gender as an integral principle in understanding migrant performers' experiences. It deeply shapes the borders of the rural–urban divide, ethnicity, and the ways in which these borders are always intersecting and mutually constitutive. In this chapter, I will first draw on a young woman informant's hospitalization experience to illustrate how her experiences of bordering are inherently gendered, and how these gendered bordering processes keep rendering her out of place. Gendered bordering processes also proliferate in migrant performers' daily work. I discuss in what ways ethnic performance is a form of sexualized labour, and detail female workers' ambivalence about undertaking such labour. The influence of work extends to female workers' non-work spheres, as it shapes their intimate negotiations with significant others. Therefore, female workers refer to certain aspects of 'ethnic scripts' to try to reframe the meaning of their labour. While male workers seem to be less troubled by undertaking sexualized labour, they use different ways to reassert their masculinity, which is arguably challenged by undertaking feminized service work. This chapter further seeks to explore the meaning of encounters with the gendered bordering processes of the rural–urban divide and ethnicity for ethnic performers.

Gendered experience of being 'out of place'

I would like to start the chapter with the story of a young woman informant named Ying, who was 17 when she first migrated to Green City. Ying worked as a performer at Waterfall Restaurant for three months. Her first-time migration experience was a short-lived one, unexpectedly ended by a sudden illness. Ying's experience of illness embodies multiple borders that migrant workers encounter, and it also shows how such experiences are inherently gendered. At the same time, it reveals how migrant women's sexualities are deemed to be 'out of place', are assigned moral value, and are therefore under constant scrutiny.

One day, when I woke up, I got several messages from co-workers at Waterfall Restaurant, saying that Ying had been sent to the hospital the night before due to an intense abdominal pain. I decided to visit her that morning instead of going to work in the restaurant. When I arrived at the hospital, I was surprised to find out that Ying had been sent for surgery, as the doctor had identified a tumour in one of her ovaries. While she was in surgery, I met Ying's aunt, Zhen, a young woman who was also a migrant worker in Green City. As it was Ying's first experience of migrating out to work, Ying's parents had asked Zhen to look after Ying whenever she could. Zhen said that Ying's parents were on their way to Green City. What seemed to worry Zhen more than the illness itself were the connotations associated with the illness. She said to me worriedly, "She [referring to Ying] is still a virgin. I know that she is – she has never been in a relationship before … How can you get such illness [in the ovary] as a virgin? It doesn't make sense to me." Later in our conversation, I began to understand why Zhen was so anxious about this particular illness. Zhen was worried that people back home would gossip about Ying's illness, and attribute the illness to her promiscuous conduct in the city despite the fact that she was still a virgin. This would – in Zhen's mind – impede Ying's future prospects of finding a good partner for marriage.

Zhen's worry is not without reason. Migrant women's sexuality is under strict scrutiny, especially when they are young, single, and migrating alone. Their sexuality is also regarded as 'potentially threatening to urban sexual mores and to state population-control policies' (Friedman, 2010: 160). As a result, migrant women are subject to scrutiny of their 'virtuous reputation' based on their sexuality (Gaetano, 2004, 2008), and have to navigate a context in which mobility is associated with immorality. It is in such a context that some migrant women choose to work as domestic workers, as the interior spaces are regarded as safe and good for their reputations (Gaetano, 2008; Jacka, 2009). In contrast, for women who work in entertainment and service work, the association between their mobility and immorality can be particularly strong (see, for example, Zheng, 2007; Otis, 2011), making workers feel the need to constantly defend their virtuous reputations in many ways.

Despite the fact that China is witnessing a shift to a more liberal culture and more diverse practices and representations about sex (Farrer, 2014), women's reputations and morality are still largely attached to their sexuality (Liu, 2016; Xie, 2021). This may be because sexuality is celebrated as an individual pursuit, which is tightly related with consumerism and the market economy, while gender as a critical category of inquiry is marginalized (Evans, 2008). More specifically, to marginalize gender as a critical lens to address issues in relation to sexuality is to ignore the unequal relations between men and women, with 'sex and sexuality becoming components of individual exploration, dissociated from broader issues of power and injustice' (Evans, 2008: 378). The marginalization of gender in discussions of sex and sexuality is partly due to how feminism is framed as a dangerous 'foreign concept' (Woodman, 2019), and how feminist activism continues to be suppressed by the state (see Fincher, 2016). Also, while research has suggested a more relaxed sexual culture in urban areas (Farrer, 2014), there is little research about the sex culture in rural China, where the underlying norms regarding women's chastity may remain largely unchanged. Therefore, rural women may find themselves under more scrutiny in relation to their chastity, especially when they migrate out alone as young single women.

Ying is not the only one who was judged on her virtuous reputation in relation to chastity. A married woman, Meihua, also mentioned that one of the reasons that she decided to migrate together with her husband was to avoid the potential stigmatization of migrating out alone by herself. Na, a female performer in Forest Park in her 20s, shared similar concerns. She mentioned how she would deliberately dress in a more conservative way when going back home, and that she was very alert about the people who 'talked behind her back'. Despite the fact that she has been cohabiting with her boyfriend for over a year in Green City, she insisted on sleeping in separate rooms when they visited Na's home. Once, when she sent extra money home compared to the usual amount of remittance, her father called her immediately. Sounding angry, he asked her why she would suddenly have all that money, and asked her if she was involved in some illicit work (implying sex work). In such a context, women like Meihua and Na, who work in sexualized ethnic performance work, feel the pressure to constantly defend their virtuous reputations.

Returning to Ying's story, her experience of being ill also vividly shows how she encountered the bordering of the rural–urban divide and ethnicity, and how such encountering is always gendered. *Hukou*, as a form of more tangible border that shapes the rural–urban divide (see Chapter 3) was encountered through Ying's in-hospital experience as well.

Later that night, I visited the hospital again to see Ying. She was out of surgery and asleep, and I met Ying's parents, who had arrived from a village about 100 miles from Green City. Ying's mother said bitterly, "I told her not to go [migrate out to work], because she is too young, but she insisted. Look how she ends up like this." She seemed to share Zhen's worries about

Ying's reputation and future prospects. Earlier in the interview, Ying said to me that she had decided to migrate out to find work mainly because she wanted to reject an arranged marriage. The man, who was much older than she was, was often present in her home, trying to persuade her and her parents to approve their marriage. Like many other migrant women, going out to work became a way for Ying to postpone marriage and gain autonomy as a wage earner (Gaetano and Jacka, 2004).

I visited Ying in the hospital again on the next day. Only Ying's mother was there this time. She said that Ying's father had gone to their town's hospital in order to get some kind of proof that the hospital in Green City required so that medical insurance would cover some of the medical bills. This was because Ying's *hukou* was not in Green City, which meant that she could not use medical insurance directly without having to go through a complicated procedure. Although Ying's father had travelled for four hours in order to get the proof from the hospital in their home town, the hospital refused to provide such proof without seeing the patient. Nobody seemed to be equipped with the knowledge of what to do in such a situation, especially under the opaque *hukou* system in Green City (see Chapter 3). Ying's parents therefore decided to transfer her to their local hospital as soon as they could to avoid a heavy medical bill that they would find difficult to handle.

Ying's struggle to find a place which recognized her access to medical insurance shows the non-portability of social welfare in China. That is to say that the localized characteristic of the social welfare regime, which is largely sustained by the *hukou* system, means that one's social welfare can only be recognized in the local area where one's *hukou* lies, and cannot be transferred and recognized elsewhere (see Shi, 2012; Lin and Mao, 2022a). Many other informants mentioned that they do not dare to go to hospital when they are sick during their *dagong* journeys. Some informants also mentioned their experience of having to go home immediately for major treatment when they were working in other provinces. Therefore, Ying's experience is not exceptional, as the same concern about the non-portability of social welfare is a much wider issue that concerns many migrant workers in China. At the same time, the localized social welfare regime also contributed to her 'out-of-placeness' – a point I will return to in the following theorization.

As Ying would not be able to keep working in Waterfall Restaurant, Ying's parents asked me to return her ethnic minority costume to her workplace and try to get her deposit back from Ms Yang. As mentioned in Chapter 2, every worker has to hand in half of their monthly wage as a form of deposit to the restaurant owner. This has become a way for the restaurant owner to exercise certain forms of control in terms of workers' performance and mobility. At that point, Ms Yang said something to me which has left a deep impression on my mind. Taking the costume from me, and handing me Ying's deposit, she said:

'I have meant to fire her [Ying] for quite some time. She must be an ethnic minority who hasn't really been outside before. She often dresses in a sloppy way, and she speaks with such strong accent ... I doubted that she would understand the customer's orders correctly or respond to their needs appropriately.'

Ying is registered as Hani, although she does not identify herself as an authentic ethnic minority person, since she does not have a great deal of understanding about this identity (see discussions in Chapter 4). However, even though Ying is an ascribed ethnic minority, the fact that she was perceived by the business owner and other people as one meant that she was subject to the same marginalization that applies to 'authentic' minority people. Again, Ying seemed to be 'out of place' because of her perceived ethnicity. Although Ying's young and exotic body was deemed desirable in ethnic performance, she was constantly deemed the embodiment of low *sushi* – judged by her accent, way of dressing, and other social characteristics. Therefore, she was desirable and disposable at the same time: the *hukou* system means that only her labour is desired in the city, but not her presence.

To reflect on Ying's experience, as a young woman, at the age of 17, she migrated out to work mainly to escape the patriarchal system of an arranged marriage, only to find herself being out of place because of the *hukou* system and her perceived ethnicity. Even her illness risked her being heavily stigmatized, because it was related to her chastity, on which she was being judged by the wider society.

Here, 'out-of-placeness' has multiple layers of meaning. It firstly refers to how *hukou* as a bordering mechanism brings 'differential inclusion' (Mezzadra and Neilson, 2013) which makes migrant workers' labour desirable, but not their presence. The localized character of citizenship in China means that one's entitlement is only recognized within a locality – mainly the place where one's *hukou* is registered (Woodman, 2018). As a migrant whose mobility is incompatible with the sedentary assumption behind the citizenship logic, Ying could not access the social welfare regime in Green City, nor could she get her entitlement to access medical insurance recognized. Secondly, as a young, single woman who migrated out alone, Ying was 'out of place', since she did not fit within the gender norms of the rural or the urban. While the urban is witnessing a shift to a more relaxed sex culture which normalizes premarital sex (Farrer, 2014), rural women are still largely valued based on their chastity. As a result, Ying's migration as a young and single woman meant that her chastity was constantly under scrutiny. Also, migrant women like Ying have to navigate sexuality and gendered borders between the rural and the urban and struggle to fit with the gender norms of either place. Thirdly, despite Ying's ambivalence about her ethnicity, the fact that she was regarded as an 'authentic' ethnic minority meant that she was deemed as 'out of place', since an ethnic minority's 'right place' is assumed to be in the remote, mountainous rural villages, rather than the urban setting. Her embodied characteristics such as accent and ways of conduct seemed to reaffirm her 'out-of-placeness' and low *suzhi* (see Sun, 2009).

Ying's experience also points to the ways that migrant performers' experiences of encountering multiple borders through migration are always gendered. Meanwhile, gender intersects with other forms of inequalities, such as the rural–urban divide and ethnicity. Migrant performers encounter these intersecting borders not just through migration, but also through their everyday work. In the following sections, I will explore how undertaking sexualized ethnic performance has different implications for male and female performers, and how they cope differently. Firstly, I will explore in what ways ethnic performance is a form of sexualized labour.

Undertaking sexualized labour

In Chapter 2, I pointed out the ways that ethnic performance can be theorized as a site in which rural, ethnic performers encounter urban, Han customers. Such encounters are intimate, not just because of the nature of interactive service work, which involves closely proximate interaction. It is also because of how performers' emotional and aesthetic labour is used to create a sense of intimacy at guests' banqueting tables. A certain amount of bodily contact is also involved in *bancan* (accompanying meals), including massaging guests' shoulders, having cross-cupped wine with guests, and sitting on VIP guests' laps in Forest Park. It is fair to say that ethnic performance is heavily sexualized, and such sexualized work sometimes leads to sexual harassment in the workplace. In this section, I will firstly discuss why and how ethnic performance is sexualized.

Ethnic performance as sexualized labour

In her work about Asian manicurists in Korean nail salons in the USA, Kang (2003) proposes the concept of 'racialized sexualization' to refer to how certain types of bodily labour performed by certain groups of people are sexualized because of the historical and cultural construction of race. The mundane and routine work of manicures performed by Asian women is imbued with sexual meanings according to the workers, customers, and public perceptions because of the racial meanings attached to Asian women in America. Kang's (2003) work highlights how race intersects with gender to shape sexualization at work.

In a similar vein, in the case of ethnic performance, the meaning of ethnicity contributes to the sexualization of ethnic performance. Also, the sexualized dimensions of ethnic scripts are often actively used by market actors to make profits. I have already discussed in the previous chapter the meaning of ethnic scripts which sexualize ethnic minority women, especially in the context of Southwest China. The portrayal of minority women as child-like, primitive yet erotic, and subject to different moral standards regarding their sexuality has been extensively discussed in academic work (see, for example, Gladney, 1994; Schein, 2000; Walsh, 2005). The social construction of minority women as more sexually open is based on the grounds that they are not subjected to the same moral code that constrains Han women's sexuality (Gladney, 1994). Such eroticized representations can also be related to the image of minority women as sexually dangerous and mysterious; for example, Miao women are believed to have the ability to use 'Gu' – sorcery – to win their loved one's favour (Schein, 2000). In this case, regardless of whether performers are authentic minority people, when they dress up and perform as ethnic minorities they are subjected to further sexualization. This again shows the ways that the boundaries of sexuality and the boundaries of ethnicity are closely intertwined and mutually constitutive (Nagel, 2000).

In her book *Markets and Bodies*, Otis (2011) talks about how female workers in a hotel in Kunming try to distinguish themselves from sex workers through a variety of means. Their presence is readily sexualized even before they have had any interaction with guests, since Yunnan is largely associated with erotic ethnic tourism, and these female workers (being seen as backward and primitive ethnic minorities regardless of their real identities) are often seen as sexually available. Therefore, female workers use 'virtuous professionalism' to distinguish themselves from sex workers, and to emphasize the professional aspect of their work (Otis, 2011). Working under similar conditions, female performers in this research share similar concerns, since they are also being sexualized, especially when they are performing as 'authentic' ethnic minorities.

At the same time, crossing the invisible yet powerful boundary of the rural–urban divide also means crossing sexual boundaries. Although rural women are often regarded as pure, simple, and vanguards of traditional values, their migration, especially if they migrate alone, provokes doubt about, and scrutiny of, the morality of their sexual conduct, as Ying's story reveals. In a sense, the sexualization of female workers as waitresses and performers is further legitimized by their social positions as 'the rural', 'the ethnic' others, and therefore 'out of place'. These views all contribute to how they are readily sexualized even before interacting with guests.

The work settings and contents of ethnic performances are scripted according to the ethnic scripts which eroticize minority women. In Waterfall Restaurant, there are multiple pictures hanging on the walls showing images of minority women dressed in revealing clothes, some of them bathing under waterfalls. In Forest Park, a typical *bancan* starts with introductory lines from the host, who is also one of the ethnic performers. These introductory lines involve jokes to create a fun and relaxing vibe, usually including depicting minority people as passionate and quick to fall in love with other people. The songs and dances that are performed are also mainly about the romantic relationships of ethnic minority people, of which the usual image is of a young woman who has fallen in love and is waiting for her lover to visit her. The design and content of ethnic performance shows how ethnic scripts deeply shape the ways that ethnic performances are conducted.

Having imagined in many ways what performance work might look like, it was still quite shocking for me when I was working as a performer myself, standing with other performers in front of guests' banqueting tables wearing short skirts in minority custom styles. I soon learnt that some guests are easier to deal with than others – female guests often request less service than male guests. Once, after performing for a table with mostly drunk male guests, they refused to let us leave. A man insisted that he would choose the most beautiful girl to massage his shoulders when doing the toasting ritual. Jiang, the leader of waitresses' team, jokingly said, "That's fine. You can choose any girl you want. We are all available – either single or divorced." All the guests laughed. There was another time when I was waiting tables together with Xiaomi and Xiaoqing. As we were standing there waiting for guests to call upon us if they needed anything, some male guests started talking to us. They asked where we were from, and whether we were single. A man, who was a businessman in Guangxi Province, jokingly said to Xiaomi, "Beauty (*meinü*), you should just follow me to Guangxi." Xiaomi replied, "No problem, ask me again later when I finish the shift." Apparently the guest found such a humorous response satisfying.

From these two cases, we can see that female workers usually feel compelled to respond to male guests' sexual attention – that includes flirting, answering awkward questions, or listening to dirty jokes. It is common in sexualized service work that women are expected to respond to these sexual attentions in various ways (Adkins, 1995). This is not usually recognized as work, as it is often regarded as women just being themselves (Hall, 1993; Adkins, 1995; Coffey et al, 2018). Sometimes workers use humour to respond in a way that will not necessarily annoy the guests. Female workers also learn to respond in such a way that ensures that the guests do not lose face (*diu mianzi*). This echoes with Otis's (2011) research about migrant female workers in luxury hotels in China, for whom not letting the guests lose face has become a way waitresses justify their compromises during work.

The sexualized working environment also legitimates and normalizes sexual harassment, even though 'sexual harassment' is a phrase that is largely absent when informants are articulating their experiences. Owning the phrase 'sexual harassment' is crucial for women to articulate their experiences and realize that they are not alone in enduring this type of behaviour (Muta,

2008). However, none of the female workers particularly used the phrase to express their concerns, whether in daily life or in interviews. This does not mean that they do not have concerns with such issues, however.

I myself experienced sexual harassment during work at Waterfall Restaurant. Once, a drunk male customer touched my body after I served him. I was angry and shocked but suddenly did not know what to do. Dressed in my working costume, I felt powerless to confront the customer. As a researcher, I was worried that if I reacted in any other way, I would be suspended from doing fieldwork there. I immediately walked out of the compartment. It was the end of the banquet anyway, and I did not have to serve him anymore. Many performers were present and witnessed this scene, as it occurred after the toasting ritual. None of them said anything to me during or after the service. In general, it seems normalized for performers to experience or witness sexual harassment at work. When I talked to one of my close colleagues at Waterfall Restaurant, she just said that it happens with drunken customers. She told me to be more careful next time.

Unlike workers in some Western countries, who can turn to managers for support when experiencing sexual harassment (see, for example, Coffey et al, 2018), there is no workplace regulation that protects workers against it in China. More importantly, the silence about sexual harassment in the workplace is connected to China's general handling of, and the political environment surrounding, sexual harassment and feminist activism at large. In 2015, during International Women's Day, a number of feminists were detained because they were planning to give out stickers about sexual harassment to raise public consciousness. Among them, five feminists were jailed, and only released one month later because of international pressure. They are being called China's Feminist Five (Fincher, 2016). Discussions regarding the need to establish specific laws against sexual harassment existed long before 2015; however, the current laws which prohibit sexual harassment in the workplace are poorly implemented and do not provide clear definitions regarding what constitutes sexual harassment (The National Law Review, 2019). Moreover, in 2018, while the #MeToo movement was sweeping across many countries and areas, China's #MeToo movement was heavily censored and suppressed by the authorities (The New York Times, 2018). Numerous online posts were deleted, and the hashtag #MeToo was removed. Moreover, mostly urban, educated young women were involved in #MeToo, and it failed to reach the millions of female migrant workers.[1] With the authorities failing to address the issue of sexual harassment, and their constant suppression of online and offline activities in addressing this issue, it is not surprising that sexual harassment was generally experienced by female workers in this study and had not yet been voiced.

While sexualized labour like ethnic performance is increasingly used to make profits, discussion and actions about gender inequality and gender-based violence are suppressed at the institutional and societal level. This enables sexual harassment to be prevalent in workplaces, and women have to bear the consequences and potential stigmatization of it. Therefore, while 'ethnic scripts' readily sexualize ethnic performances, female performers lack ways to articulate sexual harassment or to seek institutional protection. Nevertheless, they resist the stigmatization of undertaking sexualized labour in creative ways. I will talk about these ways of resistance after discussing another important reason that ethnic performances are highly sexualized. I argue that this is closely related to the banqueting culture and political environment in China. Female performers' sexualized labour is utilized to do 'distinction work' (Hanser, 2008), that is, to make guests feel entitled, and to create a sense of intimacy at the banqueting tables.

Doing 'distinction work' and creating intimacy at the banqueting tables

The sexualization of female performers is actively promoted by the work regime, as female workers' sexualities and gendered performances are used as resources to make privileged guests feel entitled and their social status recognized. As Hanser (2008) suggests, among service encounters, 'distinction work' needs to be done by workers to acknowledge guests' entitlement and distinct positions, and this eventually contributes to the social construction and reproduction of 'class'. It is also well recognized that 'distinction work' is largely reliant on female workers' sexualities and gendered bodies, as gender has become 'a powerful way of "speaking", or making, class distinctions' (Hanser, 2005: 588). In a similar sense, the ways that female performers do 'distinction work' are also largely related to their sexualized and aesthetic bodies. Such distinction work is easier to understand when put into the context of banqueting politics in China.

Once, when I was chatting with Lei, the leader of the performers' team in Forest Park (a young woman in her 30s, who was not involved in performance itself, but was in charge of managing the performers' team), she said to me:

> 'To tell you the truth, it may seem like the important bit of performance is about on-stage shows for the tourists. However, the actual key point is about *bancan* [accompanying meals], especially the *bancan* for our VIP clients. That is why I can't emphasize *yanzhi* too much when we are recruiting new performers.'

'*Yanzhi*' literally means that a person's degree of good looks can be calculated into numerical values. Lei's emphasis on performers' aesthetic appearances is closely related to how the company is using performers' aesthetic and sexualized labour to attract potential guests, and to make distinguished guests, the VIP clients, feel entitled.

The close connection between aesthetic labour and sexualized labour has been pointed out in previous research, as aesthetic labour can 'extend to sexualised labour through organisational demand for corporate "looks"' (Warhurst and Nickson, 2009: 1). Here, a particularly noteworthy point is how young migrant women's yearning to become modern citizens is also closely related to the aesthetic labour that they do at work. This means that their efforts to become figures that conform to urban beauty standards can be turned into a form of aesthetic labour at work. In Chapter 2, I talked about how young migrant women embrace consumption to aspire to become modern and urban citizens. They spend a lot of hard-earned money on cosmetic products and fashionable clothes in order to achieve urban standards of beauty. Just as women are disciplined by their femininity in factory settings (Pun, 2005), young women's self-transforming efforts are also utilized as a form of aesthetic labour in service work (Otis, 2016). The emphasis on aesthetic appearance at work has also, in turn, motivated female performers to invest more in improving their appearances. Therefore, the meaning of performers' aesthetic work is closely entangled with the meaning of the rural–urban divide and ethnicity. The aesthetic labour one does for work and for the project of self are intricately linked; this, again, points to the blurred boundaries between work and non-work spheres.

How does the performers' aesthetic and sexualized labour contribute to boosting VIP clients' experiences in Forest Park? With the progress of my fieldwork, I gradually got to know that one of the ways to provide a distinction service to VIP guests is by doing some special 'rituals' during the toasting process – female performers are requested to sit on male guests' laps while forcing wine down their throats. It is a special part of the performance which would not normally be performed for ordinary guests like tourist groups. As such performances for VIP clients are conducted in individual compartments I did not get the access needed to actually observe them. However, the fact that I was excluded from such observations is revealing in itself, as it is related to the politics of banqueting and sexual politics in China at large.

In ethnic performance, the commercialization of intimacy is evident. As Zelizer (2000) rightly points out, money does not necessarily 'corrupt' intimate relationships, rather, economic activities are central to the function of all kinds of intimate relationships, including coupling, childcare, elderly care, and so on (Zelizer, 2000). In a way, guests and tourists are 'purchasing intimacy' by requiring ethnic performances – a kind of intimacy that is crucial to facilitate business deals and political *'guanxi'* among government officials and businessmen (Zelizer, 2000; Osburg, 2013; Uretsky, 2016). This is the reason that the most intimate performances take place in private VIP rooms, with performers working their hardest trying to entertain guests, who are mostly businessmen, government officials, and their friends.

As Ho and colleagues (2018) insightfully point out, the commodification of sex is closely related to the national economy and politics. Therefore, it is essential to understand the politics of sexuality in China, otherwise it would be difficult to understand the controversy that, since the establishment of the PRC, commercialized sex is legally banned yet it is still flourishing (Ho et al, 2018). The politics of the sex industry in China, they argue, prominently shows how the sex industry has become an indispensable force to boost the national economy – not only because of the profits directly gained from the sex industry, but also because of the business deals that are facilitated and agreed upon due to the commercialization of sex (see, for example, Zheng, 2006; Osburg, 2013; Ho et al, 2018). As economic growth is often used to justify the legitimacy of the governance regime in the PRC, the tolerance of commercialized sex has political meanings. That is one of the reasons that it is mostly the 'low end' kind of commercial sex that is being suppressed by the 'sweep away yellow movements' (anti-vice campaigns), while the 'high end' sex industry is left intact (Ho et al, 2018). While what kind of effect Xi's austerity campaign has had on the sex industry since 2013 is left under-theorized, it can be speculated that commercialized sex might take more discreet forms. For example, while lavish banqueting is still essential in facilitating *guanxi*, less visible sexualized entertainment may be taking its place (Ho et al, 2018).

Ethnic performance in *bancan* is an example of how sexualized entertainment has taken a more discreet form. It is not just a coincidence that ethnic performance has flourished in the past three or four years – this is related to Xi's austerity campaign. Local government officials and public servants have been banned from going to karaoke bars and other entertainment sites. During my fieldwork, I saw government officials and businessmen taking their business deals to Waterfall Restaurant or Forest Park, especially if the guests were non-locals and they wanted to let guests experience the *minzufengqing* (ethnic flavour) of the banquets. Indeed, this seems like a safe option, since promoting ethnic culture is politically correct in China, as celebrating multi-ethnic culture reaffirms the sovereignty of the PRC.

I was not surprised, therefore, when I was informed that I was not permitted to observe what happened in the VIP compartments. It also seemed logical that staff in Waterfall Restaurant were forbidden to use mobile phones at work on the grounds that "guests would feel unease if they knew that staff could take out a mobile phone and take photos of them".[2] According to the restaurant owner, this was a request that was specifically brought up by some guests. In fact, she took pride that her restaurant was able to ensure the privacy of the guests, and regarded it as one of the selling points of her business. During my observation, there were incidences nationwide involving government officials having been filmed having banquets paid for by public funds, and subsequently being punished. Banning workers from using mobile phones is one of the ways to prevent similar things from happening again, and to ensure the privacy of guests.

In these contexts – the campaign against extravagant spending and using public funds, as well as stricter surveillance of government officials – ethnic performance seems to have become a safe choice. Moreover, merit can also be claimed for promoting and celebrating multi-ethnic culture in the local area. In this way, the sexualization of ethnic performance is justified and legitimized.

However, female performers share a lot of ambivalence about doing these particular forms of ritual during toasts. In a context in which women's sexuality is highly moralized and related to their reputations (Liu, 2016), undertaking sexualized labour has certain consequences for performers. How do female workers respond? I argue that they try to desexualize such labour by referring to certain aspects of ethnic scripts that relate undertaking ethnic performance work to promoting local ethnic cultures.

Struggles and resistance: referring to the ethnic scripts

As mentioned in the previous chapter, ethnic scripts are cultural repertoires of ethnicity which people draw on to make sense of their practices of ethnicity. State discourses, media representations, and market-endorsed practices of ethnicity all constitute ethnic scripts. Sometimes multi-layered or even contradictory messages are given by these ethnic scripts, as they are being used in different ways by different actors in specific contexts. In the context of ethnic performance, as I have shown, market actors actively mobilize popular perceptions of minority women as being sexually promiscuous and available, and this has been actively promoted in the tourism business. Meanwhile, ethnic scripts in the local context also encourage people to actively promote ethnic culture and embrace and celebrate multi-ethnic cultures. This is particularly true in the local contexts where tourism has been used as one of the major strategies to achieve poverty alleviation. To put it more bluntly, it is politically correct in Green City's local context to actively celebrate and promote ethnic culture. This has also become one aspect of the local ethnic scripts. Therefore, some female performers refer to this aspect of ethnic scripts to try to legitimize and desexualize their labour:

> 'When I first saw the VIP *bancan*, with all kinds of sitting on laps and forcing wine, all kinds of things. I even saw a guest try to touch the performer. When I went back from the scene, on my way to the dorm, I hesitated. I was wondering if I had chosen the wrong job. I felt all

kinds of entanglements of thoughts in my mind, but I never told these to my family. If my parents ask what I do for work, I just say ... well, just singing to the guests, dancing. And then toasting, you can drink if you want, and you can refuse to drink as well. So my mother has never known ... it's like ... put it bluntly you were like escorting ... Anyway, sometimes things become more acceptable as time goes on, and you get used to it. Once one of my friends saw our performance, he pointed out that this job is like accompanying drinking [*peijiu*]. I said, our work is formal work [*zhenggui*], and it is protected, something like that.' (Chun, 22 years old, female, Lahu, Forest Park)

At first, I struggled to understand what Chun meant when she said that such work is 'protected'. Later, I started to realize that she was right – that this work gained its legitimacy through public endorsement and promotion, as it is part of the ethnic scripts to promote ethnic culture. When viewed from this perspective, a boundary can be drawn between legitimate ethnic performance and other types of sex-related work that are illegal and formally banned, such as escorting and prostitution. Political legitimacy and endorsement of ethnic performance enabled Chun to continue to maintain a sense of respectability. She also referenced this aspect of ethnic scripts to defend the legitimacy of sexualized ethnic performance in front of her friend. However, a conflicted feeling, even a sense of shame, lingered, as Chun chose not to tell her parents about the exact content of her work. This suggests the importance of looking at how the sexualization of women's work has had an influence on their personal relationships, an aspect which will be discussed later in this chapter.

Other performers also shared similar ambivalence about undertaking sexualized labour. Some of them mentioned how different aspects of ethnic scripts are used to desexualize the labour:

'[In terms of sitting on guests' laps] I shouldn't have minded it because it is minority culture, it is what the previous generation of performers kept telling us. But ... I may not care as a minority person, but I would care as a woman.' (Yun, 23 years old, female, Wa, Forest Park)

'There's nothing wrong with rubbing guests' shoulders I think. It's part of our local ethnic culture, and the whole toasting process is to show hospitality to the guests – as they are often being shown in the real minority's villages.' (Mei, 30 years old, female, Han, Waterfall Restaurant)

Yun and Mei's reflections also reveal how different aspects of ethnic scripts are referred to in this particular context. By framing sitting on guests' laps as a way for simple and pure (*chunpu*) minority people to show their hospitality to guests, performers manage to downplay the sexual connotations of this performance ritual. For example, according to this logic, rubbing shoulders and sitting on laps are just ways of showing hospitality, such as minority people would do when greeting guests. Any attempt to associate sexual meanings with such practices was to contaminate the pure intentions of minority people, and to diminish the cultural significance of minority rituals.

Besides, as the development of ethnic culture has been so tightly linked with local economic development, the local ethnic scripts encourage one to broadcast ethnic culture, and even to actively commodify one's ethnicity. Therefore, promoting local ethnic culture, again, is being used to give legitimacy to the labour.

Indeed, 'it is minority culture/custom' is a popular saying when people are talking about ethnic performance. It sometimes becomes the weapon for performers' resistance and attempts to achieve an inversion of power relations. For example, guests would sometimes require performers to perform another round of toasting. In order to try to avoid this, performers would try their best to make guests drink as much as possible in the first round. They taught me to fill the guests' drinking cups with as much strong liquor as possible. And when the guests objected and said that there was too much for them to drink, performers would say things like: "That is our minority culture, and you should respect minority customs", or "You can't stop drinking until the song is over, it is our ethnic tradition." Most guests would be compelled to finish their strong alcoholic drinks and would not normally request another round of toasting. In this way, performers manage to bring a swifter end to the encounters they find awkward. By referring to such ethnic scripts, and by being in charge of urging guests' drinking, an inversion of the power relations between performers and guests is achieved temporarily.

It is revealing that while ethnic scripts legitimize the sexualization of ethnic performance, female performers also actively refer to certain aspects of ethnic scripts to desexualize the intimate rituals and practices of accompanying guests, such as by re-framing bodily contact with the guests as ethnic minority people showing their hospitality rather than as undertaking sexualized labour. In this way, female performers manage to maintain their respectability to an extent. This again points to the multi-layered meaning of ethnic scripts. It shows how ethnic scripts can not only be constraining and repressive, but can also empower people when used in certain ways. As a result, migrant women constantly struggle with different versions of ethnic scripts, which may be in conflict with each other, and provide different meanings regarding being good women and being good ethnic minorities. This reveals the nature of ethnic scripts as being multidimensional and therefore needing to be understood in relation to their specific contexts. Further, the fact that migrant women need to constantly do more work to avoid being seen as sexually promiscuous also points to 'the multiplication of labour' (Mezzadra and Neilson, 2013; Mao, 2021), although, again, such labour is not recognized or being financially remunerated.

So far, female performers' experiences have been addressed in relation to the ways that they experience sexualized labour, while male performers' voices seem to be neglected. Do male performers experience sexualization at work in the same way? In the following section, men's experiences of undertaking gendered service work will be explored.

Masculine compromise at work

In *Masculine Compromise*, Choi and Peng (2016) convincingly showed how migrant men need to compromise their masculinity in various ways as rural–urban migration has provided them with a different context, especially highlighting the contrast between their dominance in rural China versus their marginalization in the urban area. While these men see a particular version of masculinity as desirable, in reality, they have to adopt another set of practices which is not in accordance with their ideal masculinity. Whether these changing practices may lead to a changing ideology about masculinity and gender relations is a question that remains to be answered. While these masculine compromises are mainly talked about in relation to the family sphere – such as the gendered division of labour at home – the roles at work are less addressed. Do migrant men also have to compromise their masculinity at work? Research in factory settings has shown that migrant men are pushed to deal with their compromised masculinity in the workplace, since the factory work regime favours the labour of rural women (Kim, 2015; Tian and Deng, 2017). Less research focuses on such negotiations in the context of service work in China (but see Choi, 2018; Shen, 2019). As being employed in service work is regarded as 'women's work' by popular perception, as well as by most male informants themselves, it is important to understand how male workers experience this feminized and sexualized labour, and whether they experience it in similar ways to female performers. Moreover, while most migrant men are making compromises in order to continue to be the breadwinners in their families, the same is not true of young and single men like my informants. How, then, might young men defend their potentially challenged masculinity?

Most male performers in this research feel that their masculinities are more or less challenged by undertaking service work, and some of them even respond to such challenges by changing jobs. Xiaobai is one of them. He used to work in Waterfall Restaurant as a performer/waiter, but that only lasted for several days. When asked about the reason why he quit that job so quickly, he said: "It's just not gonna work well." "Why?" I asked. He paused for a little while "... because, you know, it is not a proper job for a man [*Dui yi ge da nanren lai shuo bu he shi*]." I tried to determine what the rationale behind this statement was, but Xiaobai insisted that, "It is just what it is." While it is possible that Xiaobai did not want to elaborate this point because he believed that, as a woman researcher, I could not empathize with him, it is also possible that he thought that service work was fundamentally feminized and could therefore potentially threaten his masculinity. The qualities of 'care' and 'emotionally attending to others' needs' behind service work are usually associated with femininity, and could be part of the reason that Xiaobai rejected such employment. After quitting that job, Xiaobai tried different kinds of jobs, such as working in a garage, courier services, and so on, but at the time of the interview, he was working for an advertising agency, and his work entailed erecting billboards alongside the street – a manual job that requires physical strength and endurance.

Then what about those men who continued to work as performers/waiters? Some informants defended their masculinity by referring to gendered divisions of labour at work. For instance, they would emphasize the heavy lifting part of their labour – the physical work that requires the use of bodily strength that they think women cannot manage. Interestingly, some of them also referred to gendered ways of doing emotional labour as a way to defend their masculinity:

Cheng: Like … here … [pause] … things that you do in private compartments, such as serving wine and changing small plates, they feel like … like … meticulous work [*xi huo*] … so they really seem like … not right work for us [men]. Then … sometimes guests would lash out their temper on you, and you just have to take it. They wouldn't do the same if they were male guests being served by female waitresses. (Cheng, 21 years old, male, Han, Waterfall Restaurant)

Just like the male workers in factories who are exploring a gendered labour regime which favours female workers (Kim, 2015; Tian and Deng, 2017), Cheng finds himself navigating a service work context which favours female workers rather than male workers. He is also very aware of how gender shapes his interactions with guests. As the rules of gendered interaction may allow guests to be angry at men, but it is less acceptable for them to display anger at women (Goffman, 1976), male guests do gender-specific emotion work when interacting with service workers. Cheng is able to take pride in the fact that he can endure guests' gendered displays of temper, and such endurance is thought to be related to masculinity. Therefore, by pointing out the guests' gendered displays of anger, and how he is able to 'take it', Cheng distances himself from female workers who do service work, and in this way, defends his masculinity.

The gendered division of labour also shows through in the performances. During on-stage performances, male performers tend to perform the hyper-masculine image of minority men, who used to rely on hunting to feed their families. When they are performing as lovers, they are performing the image of men who always take the initiatives in relationships, in contrast to women, who passively wait for their lovers to visit.

Moreover, some of the informants defend their challenged masculinities by emphasizing the future rather than the present. That is, many of them frame working as performers/waiters as only a temporary phase in their careers. In Waterfall Restaurant, male workers are often promoted to work in the kitchen and, if they work for some time in that position, learn 'solid' skills, but such a career path does not apply for female workers. Therefore, 'learning solid skills' (*xue yimen jishu*) had become a common goal when male informants were talking about their future plans in interviews. None of them could see themselves doing the waiting work for a long time. In fact, it is not difficult for them to be transferred to work in the kitchen after they get accustomed to waiting tables. In the kitchen, they can work their way up from bus boy to assistant chef, and then principal chef. Several male informants mentioned their plans to learn to be chefs, and then open their own small restaurants in the future. Since the staff who work in the kitchen are paid more than the waiters and waitresses, this has become a desirable choice for men to save money and learn skills for their future businesses. Some male performers also emphasize how they are cultivating skills as performers at this stage, but are aiming for a better stage or better development prospects as performers – just like the cases of Wei and Wang, discussed in the previous chapter. As cultivating skills as performers is largely incorporated in their 'enterprising selves', they tend to envision a successful future, rather than wanting to discuss the present.

More importantly, it is clear that male workers are experiencing sexualized labour in different ways than female performers. In previous sections, I have mainly talked about how female performers experience sexualization at work. It is worth pointing out that male performers, too, are expected to work as waiters catering to guests' needs. For example, during *bancan*, they are also expected to drink cross-cupped wine with female guests, as well as providing brief massages. However, none of the male performers voiced their concerns or ambivalence about doing sexualized labour in their interviews.

In my analysis, it did show that female performers are more troubled by the sexualization of work, while their male counterparts rarely mention their feelings towards the work regime. Mostly, female performers took the initiative to talk about how they were troubled by certain aspects of work, while male performers never mentioned these to me. At first, I regretted not taking the initiative to ask male informants about their feelings toward working under the sexualization of work. However, instead of regarding this silence as the absence of data, their silence or reluctance to talk about these issues may suggest that they are not troubled by it in the same way as female performers, especially when performing sexualized work is less likely to cause people to think of men as immoral or to harm their chances of marriage. It could also be because they find it difficult to express emotions in front of a woman researcher. The silence of male performers regarding undertaking sexualized labour contrasts with female performers' clearly voiced concerns and ambivalence, which suggests the need to better understand men's experiences of doing sexualized work.

While at work, migrant performers can use different ways to reassert their challenged masculinity as we have previously noted. However, their masculinity continues to be challenged outside of work, during which time they find themselves judged by the standards of 'hegemonic masculinity', which are mostly measured by their monetary power and social status. Moreover, while their female counterparts are judged because of the dubious reputation associated with doing sexualized work, male performers find themselves becoming undesirable marriage partners because of their meagre wage and lack of social status (Choi and Peng, 2016). This is also reflected in their experiences of love and romance in the city, which will be discussed in the next section.

Intimate negotiations with significant others

What does it mean for female workers to undertake sexualized work? In this section, I will try to understand this by looking at their intimate negotiations with significant others. So far, there has been relatively little work that has systematically and theoretically considered the effect of undertaking sexualized work on one's intimate relationships in China. One example would be work on the 'white collar beauties' whose sexuality is used to boost business deals but who are left vulnerable in their own intimate relationships as they are more prone to relationship breakups because of their work (Liu, 2016). However, this negotiation of the impact of work on personal lives formed only a small part of this discussion. We can also see a similar discussion concerning erotic dancers in Canada, whose full citizenship was threatened because of the work that they undertook, which positioned them 'outside of discourses that elaborated what it meant to be a normal, moral, and patriotic citizen' (Ross, 2000: 248). Moreover, the social illegitimacy of their work makes it difficult for them to enter and maintain meaningful intimate relationships with other people, making small things like picking up children at school a challenge (Ross, 2000). It might be because of similar social pressures that some female performers feel it necessary to disguise their work from significant others:

Jie: I never told him [her boyfriend] about the sitting on guests' laps part. Because he already became worried when he heard about us drinking cross-bodied wine with the guests. So I never told him there is such a thing. Although I myself do not need to do it very often because I am the host. But if he learnt that there is such an activity, he would definitely become suspicious, because he knows that if it is a thing, it will one day be my turn .... My mother was initially against it [my work]. Because I told her it is *bancan*, and she doesn't understand what it is. I said is it like catering guests [*jie dai*], to toasting to the guests. She became worried after that. She said, what? You mean you have to drink it yourself? ... Then she called me frequently during those days. She said, don't worry about the wage, if you can't take it, just go home. Even if you don't work, I can afford your expenses ... Actually in her mind, she was already ... imagining things.

Researcher: Right, she must be worried.

Jie: Yes, and then I explained to her many times that there's nothing outrageous, just singing to other people and clinking our cups. Nothing ... you know, nothing going too far. (Jie, 20 years old, female, Han, Forest Park)

Jie knows that her morality as a respectable woman is challenged by the content of her work. She responded by not discussing the details of her work with her family and boyfriend. Such disguise and self-censorship make her more vulnerable, since she has less support when she encounters hardships at work. While intimate relationships usually serve as strong support networks for migrants, Jie is intentionally distancing herself from such support because she does not want to become morally questionable in other people's eyes, or let her mother worry too much about her. It is ironic that Jie's work to contribute to guests' intimacy at banquets becomes an obstacle to her own intimacy. Distancing from significant others becomes necessary for Jie to maintain her respectability, but it comes at the price of potentially jeopardizing her own intimate relationships. As the practices of intimacy include being able to share intimate knowledge with each other (Jamieson, 2011), the inability to share things about work – which constitutes the majority of Jie's time – not only makes her more isolated from her support networks, but also affects her practices of intimacy.

Moreover, such distancing and avoidance of talking about her job does not always work well, since the stigmatization attached to sexualized performance work can be difficult to avoid. Hua, another female performer, mentioned an incident she had with her ex-boyfriend, which she thinks is related to her work. Unlike Jie, Hua chose to tell her boyfriend about what happens at work, even though she kept this secret from her parents. Hua's ex-boyfriend initially showed understanding and support for her work. However, they later got into a fierce fight, where he accused her of behaving inappropriately when she hung out with some male friends in a private setting. In their fight, Hua's work was brought up frequently, when her ex-boyfriend accused her of being 'badly influenced by her work', and of showing less respect for herself and their relationship. Hua's work became something that made her morally questionable, even when she was off work. They broke up shortly after the fight.

Hua is not the only one who is deemed less respectable and less desirable as a marriage partner because of working as an ethnic performer. When I was interviewing a male worker named Qiang in Waterfall Restaurant, he said half-jokingly, "I would never marry a girl from Waterfall Restaurant." I asked why, and he said, "I don't know how to explain. Nowadays society is so complicated ... they can be girlfriends, but definitely not the ones that you should marry." Some migrant men still value the 'rural femininity' that characterizes women as being obedient, filial, domestically oriented, simple, and chaste (Lui, 2016), and that is one of the reasons that rural migrant men usually undertake sexual adventures and experience the urban ideal of romance and intimacy in the cities, but return to their villages to marry local girls (Choi and Peng, 2016). For female performers like Hua, working in a highly sexualized setting makes one morally questionable, and no longer able to be identified with the ideals of being pure, simple, and conservative. They therefore become less desirable partners for marriage.

Qiang's feelings about how society is 'complicated' these days are shared by many male performers. They often use words like 'chaotic' (*luan*) and 'complicated' (*fuza*) to articulate this feeling. This may be because of a paradox in China's sexual culture. On the one hand, China is witnessing a shift toward a more liberal and diverse sex culture in which young people have more space to explore and express their sexualities (Farrer, 2014), but, on the other hand, with gender as a critical analytical discourse being marginalized, these more diverse sexual practices do not necessarily lead to more equal gender relationships or more fluid understandings of gender that can challenge its normative definition (Evans, 2008). This is one of the reasons that women's sexuality is still highly moralized in China. For migrant men, the more diverse sexual practices and culture, on the one hand, afford them more opportunities to experience sex and love, but, on the other hand, they increase their anxieties about finding the 'right' partner who still embodies the traditional rural femininity that is deemed desirable. Their marginalized positions make them feel more vulnerable in the dating market, and they therefore put more emphasis on qualities like 'loyalty', 'chastity', and rural femininity. Within the relationship sphere, they have different standards for 'ideal girlfriend' and 'ideal wife' (Choi and Peng, 2016). While they are open minded about their own sexual adventures, they still frown upon women who do the same thing.

Conclusion

This chapter illustrates how the lens of intimacy enables us to understand migrant performers' work and lives as governed by the gendered aspects of bordering. The ways that informants encounter bordering processes in relation to the rural–urban divide and ethnicity are deeply gendered, as shown through Ying's story, and also through male and female performers' (different) negotiations in relation to undertaking sexualized and feminized service work.

Ethnic performances are sexualized labour because of the ethnic scripts which readily sexualize ethnic minority women in Southwest China, even before the encounters between workers and guests take place. This also relates to how female performers' aesthetic and sexualized labour is used to make guests feel entitled, and to contribute to their *guanxi*-building processes at the banquets. Such a work regime also normalizes sexual harassment, especially in the context of the current political regime which constantly suppresses feminist activism.

Female workers' reputations are threatened because of the sexualized work that they undertake. This is due to the moralizing of women's sexuality and essentialized understandings of gender and sexuality. Therefore, female workers feel the need to use different ways to desexualize their labour. To be more specific, they refer to the different aspects of ethnic scripts which encourage the promotion of local ethnic culture, and frame bodily contact with guests as the practice of pure minorities showing their hospitality. In that way, female performers seek to justify the legitimacy of their labour and manage bordering between respectable and shameful womanhood.

At the same time, migrant male performers experience the sexualization of labour in different terms. Being subjected to the 'Han gaze' (Schein, 2000) does not necessarily make them feminized, and they are less affected by undertaking sexualized labour since they are not subject to the same standards of sexual morality. However, they still need to find ways to defend their masculinity from the challenges stemming from their undertaking feminized service work and their marginalized position in society. They do so by emphasizing the gendered division of labour, including manual labour that requires physical strength and gendered emotional management which enables them to manage guests who display anger to them. They also distance themselves from femininity as much as they can by doing different work or trying to avoid emotional labour. Moreover, they defend their masculinity by emphasizing the future, while depicting their current work and life situation as temporary. Some performers also cultivate their talents and ethnic selves, aspiring to future success as a performer, as mentioned in the previous chapter. Through these means, male workers defend their masculinity by referring to essentialized gender norms regarding masculinity and femininity.

Undertaking sexualized labour also overshadows female performers' intimate relationships with significant others. Some of them withhold information about work from family members, which may help them maintain their reputations, but leaves them vulnerable and with little support. They are also deemed undesirable marriage partners, and experience fights with partners because of their work. These aspects reveal how work increasingly overtakes our 'private' lives, and sheds light on the ever-more blurring boundary between work and non-work spheres.

By looking broadly at intimacy as negotiated within work as well as 'private' relationships, intimacy as a lens reveals how gender is negotiated in close association with ethnic scripts. It also reveals how it is a gendered process for a migrant worker travelling from the rural, but struggling to arrive in the urban.

6

Conclusion

This book is about what we can learn from systematically focusing on a series of negotiations which are generally conducted in 'private' spheres and considered personal, and which therefore tend to go under the sociological radar. It does so by focusing on a group of people who have received little academic attention before – migrant performers in Southwest China. As rural–urban migrants, performers' experiences are less theorized because they are intra-provincial migrants who migrate to work in an adjacent city, which is small in scale and is not a popular migration destination. Their experiences are different from the 'typical migrants' who migrate from inland, western provinces to work in the south-eastern coastal areas, where most of the Special Economic Zones are concentrated, and extensive labour forces are employed to work in manufacturing industries (making China 'the World Factory'). While in recent years the number of migrants who move within the province, and who work in the service sector, has risen rapidly, the case of ethnic performers offers new insights in understanding this under-researched group of migrants. At the same time, ethnicity remains an issue that has rarely been addressed in rural–urban migration literature. Therefore, we have a very limited understanding of how ethnic minority migrants' experiences might be different from their Han counterparts, and how ethnicity plays a role in shaping their migration experiences. This book is an attempt to bridge these gaps by focusing on the work and migration experiences of ethnic performers.

Echoing Wanning Sun's (2023) powerful advocating for an 'intimate turn' to study inequality in China, this book demonstrates the intimate consequences of social inequalities: how the multi-layered inequalities regarding the rural–urban divide, ethnicity and gender have a profound impact on ethnic performers' emotions, sense of self, and their relationships with other people. At the same time, it seeks to move beyond merely exploring the intimate *consequences* of inequalities, and further asks how we could use these intimate negotiations as a *means* to understand social inequalities – an approach I call 'intimacy as a lens'. In other words, intimacy as a lens means starting from the intimate realm and working from there to understand broader social inequalities. As this book demonstrates, the lens of intimacy provides valuable insights that otherwise tend to be overlooked, and illuminates how power and inequalities work in contemporary China.

Intimate border encounters

By adopting the lens of intimacy, this book seeks to 'use micro-scale everyday bordering practices to both conceptualise and visualise what borders are at a more general level' (Yuval-Davis, 2013: 16). Here, border is used as a concept to understand the constantly changing and unstable boundaries of social positioning —most notably for migrant performers in relation to the rural–urban divide and ethnicity. It is a move away from theorizing borders as predominantly national borders and as geographical or material forms. Rather, borders can be symbolic and ideological, and are at work 'whenever a distinction between subject and object is established' (Mezzadra and Neilson, 2013: 16). Some concepts are borrowed from *Border as Method* to understand the working mechanisms of bordering processes, which mainly include 'differential inclusion', 'the multiplication of labour', and 'border struggles' (Mezzadra and Neilson, 2013).

As argued in Chapter 2, borders proliferate in performers' everyday work firstly and foremostly because of the ways that they have to do interactive service work. In contrast to working in factories, which is the focus of the majority of research on migrant workers in China, ethnic performance is a site where performers and guests interact with each other in a physically close manner. Inspired by Hanser's (2008) work on 'service encounters', I argue that ethnic performance can be theorized as a site of encounter. As minority, rural, feminized service providers encounter Han, urban, mostly male customers, physical proximity may render their social distance even more significant. Such encounters are fleeting, but they can have profound impacts on performers' intimate negotiations. For example, the need to constantly respond to guests' comments and questions about ethnicity may serve as a 'daily reminder of ethnicity' (Bai, 2007: 257) for performers, and it may engender their reflexivity in thinking more about what ethnicity means for them.

In Chapter 2, I also explore concepts that are useful in illuminating our understanding of ethnic performance work, such as 'affective labour', 'framed by ethnicity', and 'the cultural authority of the state'. I point to the difficulty of fully capturing the multifaceted meaning of ethnic performance with one concept. Therefore, from the performers' point of view, a more useful way to understand their experiences is to understand ethnic performance as a site of encounter, and to understand what it means for performers to encounter borders in their everyday work and migration journeys. Here,

I expand the meaning of 'encounter' to include not only service encounters between performers and guests, but also the ways that performers encounter various bordering processes through their daily work and migration, most notably revolving around the rural–urban divide and ethnicity.

Chapter 3 explores in more detail performers' intimate border struggles over the rural–urban divide. *Hukou* is first and foremost an important mechanism that contributes to the construction and maintenance of the rural–urban divide. While it is often thought to be only relevant at the administrative level, the lens of intimacy reveals that informants' negotiations over *hukou* transfer decisions are highly emotional. Therefore, emotions should be taken into account in understanding 'the *hukou* puzzle' (Chen and Fan, 2016) – the fact that migrants are not always eager and willing to transfer their *hukou* to small- and medium-sized cities even when they are allowed to do so. The *hukou* puzzle was situated in the recent wave of *hukou* reform in 2014, and it is clearly applicable to the context of Green City – a small-scale city which technically allows *hukou* transfer. Such policy shifts call for more empirical data about how migrants themselves experience the loosening of *hukou* policy in small- and medium-sized cities, which remains an under-researched area. This research contributes to this gap by focusing on the types of emotional reflexivity informants engage in about *hukou* transfer decisions or imaginaries. They do not make such decisions merely on the basis of a rational calculation to maximize their profit; rather, their decision-making is shaped by their senses of entitlement, how they envision their future lives, and their life stages and relationships with significant others. Further, their emotional negotiations over *hukou* reveal the underlying logic of citizenship as a form of reward to 'successful citizens', which also regards sedentarism as the norm (Woodman and Guo, 2017; Woodman, 2018). As migrants without *hukou*, performers are subject to 'differential inclusion' in the cities: while their labour is desired as performers, their settlement in cities is largely problematized. Also, informants' emotional negotiations should be understood in relation to the emotional regime of contemporary China, which is significantly shaped by neoliberalism, emphasizing personal responsibility, happiness, and positive energies. Under such an emotional regime (Reddy, 2001), migrants tend to re-frame their 'negative emotions' into positive ones, and blame themselves for not being successful enough to earn urban *hukou*. The dominance of 'positive emotions' and the relative absence of 'negative emotions' speak volumes about the emotional regime of contemporary China.

Meanwhile, bordering processes around the rural–urban divide are not only confined to *hukou*, but also extend to other areas of life, and have intimate consequences for performers. The different meanings attached to the rural and the urban also play a significant role in informants' personhood, as they are eager to use rural–urban migration to achieve the modern and valuable personhood to which they aspire. In that sense, bordering processes also work through the cultural authority of the state (Nyíri, 2010), as different meanings are assigned to the rural and the urban, as well as to the ethnic and the Han. Ironically, while informants aspire to use mobility to achieve the modern self, they are rendered 'out of place' after their migration. Such 'out-of-placeness' is also largely related to the work that performers do, and particularly the ethnic aspect of it, which requires them to keep performing the primitive and backward images of ethnic minority people.

Therefore, ethnicity is another form of bordering process that migrant performers constantly encounter in their daily lives, which I explore in detail in Chapter 4. As performers need to dress like ethnic minority people, and have to perform ethnicity in daily work in particular ways, they have to encounter the issue of ethnicity in their daily work lives, regardless of whether they think of themselves as ethnic minorities. This book highlights the ways in which encountering ethnicity daily at work has engendered people's reflexivity about the meaning of ethnicity. By taking their ambivalences regarding whether or not they are 'authentic' ethnic minorities seriously, the important role of *practices* in people's sense of being ethnic is highlighted. Therefore, a theoretical shift from viewing ethnicity as something we are to something we do is proposed. Meanwhile, there are existing cultural norms regarding the 'right' way to do ethnicity in China, and the state's role in shaping such cultural norms is particularly strong. The idea of 'ethnic scripts' is therefore proposed to understand how informants make sense of their individual ethnicities by referring to broader normative cultural ideas about ethnicity. Such negotiations are intimate ones, as they have an impact on people's emotions and senses of self. For example, in order to achieve 'valuable personhood' (Skeggs, 2011), informants work on their ethnic selves in certain ways which accord with state and market versions of ethnic scripts. Also, ethnic scripts become part of the 'feeling rules' (Hochschild, 1979) which shape how performers manage their emotions at work in order to become happy, worry-free ethnic minorities whose ways of living are incompatible with the modern, competitive world. Ethnic scripts also sexualize minority women, as they tend to depict minority women as subject to different moral standards of sexuality than the Han. Therefore, ethnic performance also largely involves sexualized work.

In Chapter 5, I explore the different ways that female performers and male performers respond to undertaking sexualized work, and how their border encounters are always gendered. While male performers remain silent about undertaking sexualized work, female performers express concerns over doing sexualized labour. Female informants who work in sexualized ethnic performance work feel pressured to constantly defend their virtuous reputations, as they are still judged by a norm of rural femininity which emphasizes chastity. Ethnic performers undertake sexualized labour to create a sense of intimacy at guests' dining tables, which contributes to guests' *guanxi*-building processes. In some circumstances, female performers are even expected to sit on male guests' laps as a form of 'distinction work' (Hanser, 2008) to make guests feel entitled. Sexual harassment is tolerated, and even normalized, as part of the work; this is especially true in the current political context in China, which largely represses feminist activism, including arresting feminist activists and heavily censoring the #MeToo movement online. Ethnic performance work is also sexualized because of ethnic scripts which sexualize ethnic minority women, especially in the context of Southwest China. Therefore, guests already have in mind that they are going to interact with exotic and erotic minority women, even before such interactions begin. Interestingly, while, on the one hand, ethnic scripts sexualize female performers' labour, on the other hand, ethnic scripts are also drawn on by performers to re-frame the meaning of this labour. To be more specific, in the local contexts where promoting ethnic culture is closely related to economic development and poverty alleviation, local ethnic scripts encourage people to commodify their ethnicities. Female performers refer to this aspect of ethnic scripts to frame ethnic performance as 'promoting ethnic culture'. In this way, they manage to legitimize and justify doing sexualized labour by re-framing its meaning. However, undertaking sexualized labour still has an impact on performers' relationships with their significant others, as they are compelled to withhold information about their work from them in order to maintain their reputations. This has an impact on their romantic relationships as well, as some female performers are rendered undesirable marriage partners because of the work that they do. This again shows the link between work and non-work spheres, as the impact of work can extend its influence to impact on the most private and intimate negotiations. At the same time, while male performers are not sexualized in the same way as female performers, they still have to deal with the fact that they are undertaking 'feminized' service work. They respond to this in different ways. Most importantly, they aspire to future success which is largely related to money-earning abilities and hegemonic masculinity. This shows how their border encounters are always gendered.

While showing the ways that border struggles have proliferated in migrant performers' everyday work and lives, this book explores the ways that such encounters are always intimate, emotional, and personal. Also, taking a closer look at these intimate negotiations provides a valuable lens to understand the working mechanisms of borders, as well as the broader social structure. In the following section, I discuss in more detail the value of 'intimacy as a lens' as a theoretical framework.

Intimacy as a lens

This book has shown the value of the lens of intimacy as a useful approach in revealing the personal and the social. In this section, a more detailed summary will be provided in terms of what exactly the value of intimacy as a lens is, and especially how it can have dialogue with existing theoretical approaches and how it can potentially be used for future research.

The value of intimacy as a lens firstly lies in how it can bring together spheres that tend to be studied as separate fields (such as mobility, work, ethnicity, and personal life), and to see these spheres as intricately linked. It does not confine the scope of research to a certain institution, such as the family, but rather allows a more fluid investigation of intimate negotiations across different spheres. This is one way in which it resonates with the 'personal life' approach, as it allows more fluid investigations of intimacy which transcend different spheres of life and which cannot be conveniently put into boxes that suit conventional sociological categorization (Smart, 2007; May, 2011). Although using the personal as the starting point, the major departure of this approach is that it offers a more specific definition of intimacy, incorporating emotions, personhood, and relationships, while personal life may risk having too broad a focus. Also, despite the fact that the personal life approach tries to move away from the conventional approach to family life, it still (to an extent) prioritizes family lives and intimate relationships as its major foci. Therefore, without prioritizing intimate relationships, the lens of intimacy revealed the following five themes.

Firstly, one of the key themes that the lens of intimacy reveals is the intersection between work and personal life, as it shows the blurred borders between work and non-work spheres, and reveals that work has to be understood in relation to the personal lives of migrant performers. Here, 'the multiplication of labour' as a concept is useful in theorizing the ways that work intersects with informants' personal lives in various ways (Mezzadra and Neilson, 2013). Work firstly *intensifies* as it colonizes more of the informants' lives. This is not only revealed through how informants have to work for prolonged hours, but also through how work intrudes in more areas of their lives.

For example, work does not just mean how individuals can be alienated from their authentic selves (Hochschild, 1983), it also shapes their potential selves, that is, what they aspire to become (Akalin, 2007; Weeks, 2007). Informants engage in a more playful and reflexive self-making, which is nevertheless constrained by ethnicity and gender. For example, working in a context in which there are 'daily reminders of ethnicity' (Bai, 2007: 257), and in which one's ethnicity is commercialized, pushes some performers to work on their ethnic selves in order to capitalize on their ethnicities and add value to their personhood. Also, while female performers' sexualized labour is used to contribute to the intimacy at guests' banqueting tables, their own intimate relationships are compromised, as they have to hide information from their significant others and may be treated as morally questionable by their (potential) partners. While some performers escape factory work to avoid feeling like machines – as was the case with Jun, which I mentioned in the introductory chapter – in service work spheres, they are subject to different forms of exploitation which relate to their bodies, emotions, sense of self, and relationships with others.

The multiplication of labour also means that work has *diversified*, meaning that informants are expected to do multiple aspects of labour at the same time (Mezzadra and Neilson, 2013). For example, they have to do emotion work (Hochschild, 1979) according to ethnic scripts to show happy images of ethnic minorities living worry-free lives. Ethnic minority women, while doing 'distinction work' (Hanser, 2008) in recognition of the entitlement and privilege of their elite male guests, also have to do extra work to deal with the stigmatization attached to undertaking sexualized labour. Furthermore, in order to try to leave guests with the impression of meeting authentic ethnic minorities, performers have to work on their ethnic selves in certain ways to successfully satisfy 'ethnic assessment'. Many aspects of labour tend to be unrecognized and unremunerated, despite the fact that they are increasingly important parts of migrant performers' daily work.

Secondly, looking through the lens of intimacy, the ways that work shapes informants' personhood also sheds light on how we can think about personhood and self-making as relational. Contrary to the assumption that people who engage in ethnic tourism can make a clear distinction between their on-stage selves and back-stage selves (see, for example, Li, 2003; Bai, 2007), this book shows that work penetrates informants' self-making in more profound and intimate ways. This challenges the individualization thesis, which emphasizes that people have the autonomy to live their own lives without constraints from traditional social roles and structures in modernity (see, for example, Beck, 1992), and which also fails to theorize self-making in relational ways, overemphasizing people's agency, and neglects the constraints of social structures.

This book shows that to claim self-making as relational does not only mean recognizing how the self is shaped by social interactions with other people, but also requires recognizing the ways in which self-making is shaped by normative socio-cultural repertoires of meaning. The most telling examples are found in the ways that existing ethnic scripts shape the ways performers work on their ethnic selves in order to achieve 'valuable personhood'. Normative cultural ideas about the division between rural and urban also push informants to aspire to become modern urbanites through migration and consumption. While recognizing the agency that requires informants to resist social inequalities, it is also important to recognize the ways that their personhood is nevertheless constrained by social inequalities.

Thirdly, the lens of intimacy highlights the importance of using an emotionally informed approach to studying social inequalities. Existing research concerned with the emotions of rural–urban migrants in China is mainly from psychological perspectives, including major focuses on their mental health, subjective well-being, and senses of happiness (see, for example, Gao and Smyth, 2011; Cheng et al, 2014). This book approaches emotions from a sociological point of view, and regards them as a response to the ways in which people are embedded in patterns of relationships, both to others and to significant social and political events or situations (Burkitt, 2014). Also, the lens of intimacy is a departure from thinking of emotions as mere consequences of inequalities, as it also regards emotions as a tool to understand broader social issues. This means to ask not only, 'what does inequality feel like', but also, 'what do these emotions reveal?'

Using emotions as a lens firstly means to take informants' emotions seriously. By taking informants' ambivalence towards their ethnic identities seriously, this book has discovered the important role of ethnic scripts in shaping informants' practices of ethnicity. By recognizing the different emotions informants have regarding *hukou*, this book proposes answers to the *hukou* puzzle which do not assume that people make rational choices without having their actions shaped by emotions. Furthermore, informants' micro emotional negotiations also reveal the broader emotional regime of our time, which emphasizes personal responsibility, personal success, happiness, and other positive energies. The lens of intimacy also encourages researchers to theorize emotions outside relationship spheres, and the lens applies to areas which tend to be regarded as unemotional. For example, *hukou* as a form of migration regime is often thought to be relevant only in an administrative sense, but the lens of intimacy, through informants' experiences, reveals that *hukou* as a formal migration regime is fundamentally emotional.

Fourthly, intimacy as a lens allows us to understand inequalities as intersecting, while challenging the static boundaries of social categories in the intersectionality framework. One of the drawbacks of intersectionality theory is that sometimes people cannot fit neatly into a certain category which ostensibly characterizes their social positionings. McCall (2005) refers to this messy positioning as 'intra-category', seeking to problematize the very categories and boundaries of social positionings like race, class, and gender. The case of migrant performers shows exactly this instability and constant changing of boundaries, as migrant performers negotiate being rural or urban, as well as being ethnic minorities or Han. Their ambivalences over such rigid divisions show the importance of focusing on 'intra-category' positionings in intersectionality theories. While in this research I have sought to make up this limitation by adopting the concept of borders/bordering, this does not deny the fact that these inequalities do intersect with each other in various ways. Being rural is intricately linked with being ethnic, while gender plays a crucial role in shaping informants' experiences of being rural and ethnic minorities – as shown through the dilemma of female performers undertaking sexualized work.

Meanwhile, while 'class' is a word that is largely absent from this book – mainly because none of the informants ever used it to articulate their experiences – this research shows how class is being produced and reproduced even while the language of class diminishes in Chinese society. Indeed, there is 'a new Chinese working class struggling to be born at the very moment that the language of class has been sentenced to death' (Pun, 2005: 24). The silence within the language about class has been filled with new discourses such as neoliberal ones which emphasize personal responsibility, competition, and individualism (Pun, 2005). In this research, we can also see the ways that the language of class has been replaced by other vocabularies, such as the urban and the rural and the Han and the ethnic. Future research could look more closely at the ways in which people talk about class without necessarily using the word itself in contemporary China.

Fifthly, the lens of intimacy should be part of the study of the cultural politics of inequality (Sun, 2013). Forty years of reform has turned China into one of the most unequal countries in the world. While studies of inequality in China tend to focus on its economic and material forms, the important role of 'culture' should be taken into consideration (Sun, 2013). Cultural politics are essentially about meaning, but it is important to remember that meaning is not only conveyed through words and symbols (Nash, 2009). We should not neglect the ways that inequalities are felt and experienced by embodied persons with emotions:

> Although what is important in a general way in cultural politics is how symbols are interpreted and re-interpreted in social life, it is important not to lose sight of the fact that it is embodied people with emotional ties to others and individual biographies who are making social reality. (Nash, 2009: 34)

These emotions and intimate negotiations are all infused with meanings. It is vital to understand them, just like words, symbols, and rational choices. An example would be how the different emotions informants have regarding the *hukou* system are important to understand because they reveal different social meanings, such as the broader emotional regime which shapes informants' emotional reflexivity. Meanwhile, people's intimate negotiations are not just the *consequence* but sometimes also work to legitimate and maintain social inequalities. The lack of anger shown by migrants deprived of equal treatment in their own country demonstrates how such inequality becomes deeply ingrained and naturalized. Performers' aspirations to be recognized as valuable also motivate them to work on their ethnic selves in ways that sometimes further strengthens the portrayal of ethnic stereotypes. To recognize how these intimate negotiations play a role in maintaining the existing inequalities at multiple levels is an important step to take in challenging such inequalities.

In this way, the lens of intimacy requires the sociological imagination, which sees through the connections between personal biography and historical context (Mills, 2000). I find focusing on people's emotional and intimate negotiations valuable at exactly the point where I am unable to understand these private negotiations without understanding the broader context that shapes them. The lens of intimacy also blurs the boundary between the public and private. In a way, this book provides an answer to the question of what it means to say that 'the personal is political', and more importantly, illuminates how we can understand 'the political' better if we take 'the personal' seriously.

Notes

Chapter 1
1. The specific link to the media reports on this village will not be given here since this would reveal the real name of Green City.
2. This is related to the overall discrimination against LGBT people in China. See a recent review article by Wang et al, 2019.

Chapter 2
1. This involves two people linking arms to drink wine from their own cups, which is a ritual in traditional Chinese weddings that symbolizes the bride and groom bonding.
2. This is from a local news report online. The specific link will not be put here in order to ensure anonymity of the place being researched.

Chapter 3
1. See, for example: http://news.cntv.cn/2015/03/23/VIDE1427112535332815.shtml (in Chinese) [Accessed 4 December 2021].
2. Out of concern for anonymity, I shall not provide the website links here since otherwise it would make Green City identifiable.

Chapter 4
1. Elsewhere I discuss friends' crucial role in facilitating job opportunities for young migrant workers. See Mao and Yan (2023).

Chapter 5
1. Except for one case in the Foxconn factory, in which women workers raised concerns about establishing anti-harassment infrastructures. No updates were reported on this issue. See: http://en.hkctu.org.hk/content/metoo-movement-beyond-reach-china's-women-workers [Accessed 19 December 2019].
2. Quotes from field notes, from the restaurant owner Ms Yang.

References

Adkins, L. (1995) *Gendered Work: Sexuality, Family and the Labour Market*, Bristol: Open University Press.
Ahmed, S. (2010) *Melancholic Migrants: The Promise of Happiness*, Durham, NC: Duke University Press.
Ahmed, S. (2013) *Strange Encounters: Embodied Others in Post-coloniality*, London: Routledge.
Akalin, A. (2007) Hired as a caregiver, demanded as a housewife: becoming a migrant domestic worker in Turkey, *European Journal of Women's Studies*, 14(3): 209–25.
Bai, Z. (2007) Ethnic identities under the tourist gaze, *Asian Ethnicity*, 8(3): 245–59.
Barabantseva, E. (2008) From the language of class to the rhetoric of development: discourses of 'nationality' and 'ethnicity' in China, *Journal of Contemporary China*, 17(56): 565–89.
Barabantseva, E. (2010) *Overseas Chinese, Ethnic Minorities, and Nationalism De-Centering China*, Hoboken, NJ: Taylor & Francis.
Barabantseva, E. (2015) From "customary" to "illegal": Yao ethnic marriages on the Sino-Vietnamese border, *Cross-Currents*, 15: 57–81.
Barbalet, J. (2018) Guanxi as social exchange: emotions, power and corruption, *Sociology*, 52(5): 934–49.
Beck, U. (1992) *Risk Society: Towards a New Modernity*, London: Sage.
Beck, U. and Beck-Gernsheim, E. (1995) *The Normal Chaos of Love*, Cambridge: Polity Press.
Bentley, G.C. (1987) Ethnicity and practice, *Comparative Studies in Society and History*, 29: 24–55.
Boccagni, P. and Baldassar, L. (2015) Emotions on the move: mapping the emergent field of emotion and migration, *Emotion, Space and Society*, 16: 73–80.
Bourdieu, P. (1977) *Outline of a Theory of Practice*, Cambridge: Cambridge University Press.
Brownlie, J. (2011) 'Being there': multidimensionality, reflexivity and the study of emotional lives, *British Journal of Sociology*, 62(3): 462–81.

Burkitt, I. (2012) Emotional reflexivity: feeling, emotion and imagination in reflexive dialogues, *Sociology*, 46(3): 458–72.

Burkitt, I. (2014) *Emotions and Social Relations*, Thousand Oaks, CA: Sage.

Carling, J. and Collins, F. (2018) Aspiration, desire and drivers of migration, *Journal of Ethnic and Migration Studies: Special Issue: Aspiration, Desire and the Drivers of Migration*, 44(6): 909–26.

Castles, S. (1995) How nation-states respond to immigration and ethnic diversity, *Journal of Ethnic and Migration Studies*, 21(3): 293–308.

Chan, C.K.-C. and Pun, N. (2009) The making of a new working class? A study of collective actions of migrant workers in South China, *The China Quarterly*, 198: 287–303.

Chan, J. (2014) Dying for an iPhone: the labour struggle of China's new working class, *Triple C: Communication, Capitalism & Critique. Open Access Journal for a Global Sustainable Information Society*, 12(2).

Chan, J., Pun, N. and Selden, M. (2013) The politics of global production: Apple, Foxconn and China's new working class, *New Technology, Work and Employment*, 28(2): 100–15.

Chan, J., Selden, M. and Pun, N. (2020) *Dying for an iPhone: Apple, Foxconn, and the Lives of China's Workers*. Chicago, IL: Haymarket Books.

Chan, K.W. (2010) The household registration system and migrant labor in China: notes on a debate, *Population and Development Review*, 36(2): 357–64.

Chan.K.W. and Buckingham, W. (2008) Is China abolishing the hukou system? *The China Quarterly*, 195: 582–606.

Chang, L.T. (2009) *Factory Girls: From Village to City in a Changing China*, New York: Random House.

Charsley, K. and Bolognani, M. (2017) Being a freshie is (not) cool: stigma, capital and disgust in British Pakistani stereotypes of new subcontinental migrants, *Ethnic and Racial Studies*, 40(1): 43–62.

Chen, C. and Fan, C.C. (2016) China's hukou puzzle: why don't rural migrants want urban hukou? *China Review*, 16(3): 9–39.

Cheng, Z., Wang, H. and Smyth, R. (2014) Happiness and job satisfaction in urban China: a comparative study of two generations of migrants and urban locals, *Urban Studies*, 51(10): 2160–84.

China Daily (2019) China's service sector new economic growth engine, *China Daily*, 23 May. Available from: http://www.chinadaily.com.cn/a/ 201905/ 23/WS5ce60fa8a3104842260bd5d0.html [Accessed 15 November 2019].

China Labour Bulletin (2019) Migrant workers and their children. Hong Kong: China Labour Bulletin. Available from: https://clb.org.hk/content/ migrant-workers-and-their-children [Accessed 6 December 2019].

Chio, J.T. (2014) *A Landscape of Travel: The Work of Tourism in Rural Ethnic China*, Seattle, WA: University of Washington Press.

Choi, S.Y. (2018) Masculinity and precarity: male migrant taxi drivers in South China, *Work, Employment and Society*, 32(3): 493–508.

Choi, S.Y. and Peng, Y. (2015) Humanized management? Capital and migrant labour in a time of labour shortage in South China, *Human Relations*, 68(2): 287–304.

Choi, S.Y. and Peng, Y. (2016) *Masculine Compromise: Migration, Family, and Gender in China*, Oakland, CA: University of California Press.

Chu, Y. (2015) The power of knowledge: a critical analysis of the depiction of ethnic minorities in China's elementary textbooks, *Race Ethnicity and Education*, 18(4): 469–87.

Cieslik, M. (2015) 'Not smiling but frowning': sociology and the 'problem of happiness', *Sociology*, 49(3): 422–37.

Coffey, J., Farrugia, D., Adkins, L. and Threadgold, S. (2018) Gender, sexuality, and risk in the practice of affective labour for young women in bar work, *Sociological Research Online*, 23(4), pp 728–43.

Cohen, M. (1993) Cultural and political inventions in modern China: the case of the Chinese "peasant', *Daedalus* (Spring): 151–70.

Collins, F.L. (2018) Desire as a theory for migration studies: temporality, assemblage and becoming in the narratives of migrants, *Journal of Ethnic and Migration Studies: Special Issue: Aspiration, Desire and the Drivers of Migration*, 44(6): 964–80.

Davis, D. (2005) Urban consumer culture, *The China Quarterly*, 183(1): 692–709.

Ding, Y. (2017) Eating the rice bowl of youth: xiaojies' everyday self-practices as doing citizenship from the margins, *Citizenship Studies: Practicing Citizenship in Contemporary China*, 21(7): 842–59.

Dong, Y. and Goodburn, C. (2020) Residence permits and points systems: new forms of educational and social stratification in urban China, *Journal of Contemporary China*, 29(125): 647–66.

Du, H. and Li, S.-M. (2012) Is it really just a rational choice? The contribution of emotional attachment to temporary migrants' intention to stay in the host city in Guangzhou, *China Review*, 12(1): 73–93.

Du, S. (2008) 'With one word and one strength': intimacy among the Lahu of Southwest China, in W.R. Jankowiak (ed.), *Intimacies: Love and Sex across Cultures*, New York: Columbia University Press.

Ehrenreich, B. and Hochschild, A.R. (2003) *Global Woman: Nannies, Maids and Sex Workers in the New Economy*, London: Granta.

Elias, N. (1978) *The Civilizing Process, Vol. 1: The History of Manners*, trans. Edmund Jephcott, Oxford: Blackwell.

Evans, H. (2008) Sexed bodies, sexualized identities, and the limits of gender, *China Information*, 22(2): 361–86.

Farrer, J. (2014) Love, sex, and commitment: delinking premarital intimacy from marriage in urban China, in D. Davis and S. Friedman (eds), *Wives, Husbands, and Lovers: Marriage and Sexuality in Hong Kong, Taiwan, and Urban China*, Stanford, CA: Stanford University Press, pp 62–96.

Fincher, L. (2016) China's Feminist Five, *Dissent*, 63(4): 84–90.
Friedman, E. and Lee, C.K. (2010) Remaking the world of Chinese labour: a 30-year retrospective, *British Journal of Industrial Relations*, 48(3): 507–33.
Friedman, S. (2006) *Intimate Politics: Marriage, the Market, and State Power in Southeastern China*, Cambridge, MA: Harvard University Press.
Friedman, S. (2010) Women, marriage and the state in contemporary China, in Elizabeth J. Perry and Mark Selden (eds), *Chinese Society: Change, Conflict and Resistance*, London and New York: Taylor and Francis, pp 166–88.
Gaetano, A. (2004) Migrant domestic workers in post-Mao Beijing, in A. Gaetano and T. Jacka (eds), *On the Move: Women and Rural-to-Urban Migration in Contemporary China*, New York: Columbia University Press.
Gaetano, A. (2008) Sexuality in diasporic space: rural-to-urban migrant women negotiating gender and marriage in contemporary China, *Gender, Place & Culture*, 15(6): 629–45.
Gaetano, A.M. and Jacka, T. (2004) *On the Move: Women and Rural-to-Urban Migration in Contemporary China*, NewYork: Columbia University Press.
Gagnon, J.H. and Simon, W. (1973) *Sexual Conduct: The Social Sources of Human Sexuality*, Chicago: Aldine.
Gao, W. and Smyth, R. (2011) What keeps China's migrant workers going? Expectations and happiness among China's floating population, *Journal of the Asia Pacific Economy*, 16(2): 163–82.
Gaudette, P. (2013) Jembe Hero: West African drummers, global mobility and cosmopolitanism as status, *Journal of Ethnic and Migration Studies: Regimes of Mobility: Imaginaries and Relationalities of Power*, 39(2): 295–310.
Giddens, A. (1991) *Modernity and Self-Identity: Self and Society in the Late Modern Age*, Cambridge: Polity Press in association with Blackwell Publishing.
Gladney, D.C. (1994) Representing nationality in China: refiguring majority/minority identities, *The Journal of Asian Studies*, 53(1): 92–123.
Goffman, E. (1976) Gender display, in *Gender Advertisements*, London: Palgrave, pp 1–9.
Goodburn, C. (2014) The end of the hukou system? Not yet. University of Nottingham China Policy Institute Policy Papers, 2.
Grillot, C. and Zhang, J. (2016) Ambivalent encounters: business and the sex markets at the China–Vietnam borderland, in P. Nyíri and D. Tan (eds) *Chinese Encounters in Southeast Asia: How People, Money, and Ideas from China Are Changing a Region*. Seattle, WA and London: University of Washington Press.
Guo, Z. and Liang, T. (2017) Differentiating citizenship in urban China: a case study of Dongguan city, *Citizenship Studies: Practicing Citizenship in Contemporary China*, 21(7): 773–91.
Gustafsson, B. and Yang, X. (2015) Are China's ethnic minorities less likely to move? *Eurasian Geography and Economics*, 56(1): 44–69.

Hall, E.J. (1993) Smiling, deferring, and flirting: doing gender by giving 'good service', *Work and Occupations*, 20(4): 452–71.

Hanser, A. (2005) The gendered rice bowl: the sexual politics of service work in urban China, *Gender & Society*, 19(5): 581–600.

Hanser, A. (2008) *Service Encounters: Class, Gender, and the Market for Social Distinction in Urban China*, Stanford, CA: Stanford University Press.

Hardt, M. (1999) Affective labor, *Boundary 2*, 26(2): 89–100.

Harrell, S. (1995) *Cultural Encounters on China's Ethnic Frontiers*, Seattle, WA: University of Washington Press.

Harvey, D. (2005) *A Brief History of Neoliberalism*, Oxford: Oxford University Press.

Hillman, B. (2003) Paradise under construction: minorities, myths and modernity in northwest Yunnan, *Asian Ethnicity*, 4(2): 175–88.

Hird, D. (2018) Smile yourself happy: Zheng Nengliang and the discursive construction of happy subjects, in G. Wielander and D. Hird (eds) *Chinese Discourses on Happiness*, Hong Kong: Hong Kong University Press, pp 106–28.

Ho, E.L.-E. (2014) The emotional economy of migration driving mainland Chinese transnational sojourning across migration regimes, *Environment and Planning A*, 46(9): 2212–27.

Ho, P.S.Y., Jackson, S., Cao, S. and Kwok, C. (2018) Sex with Chinese characteristics: sexuality research in/on 21st-century China, *The Journal of Sex Research*, 55(4–5): 486–521.

Hochschild, A.R. (1979) Emotion work, feeling rules, and social structure, *American Journal of Sociology*, 85(3): 551–75.

Hochschild, A.R. (1983) *The Managed Heart: Commercialization of Human Feeling*, Berkeley, CA and London: University of California Press.

Hochschild, A.R. (2003) *The Commercialization of Intimate Life: Notes from Home and Work*, Berkeley, CA and London: University of California Press.

Hoffman, L. (2006) Autonomous choices and patriotic professionalism: on governmentality in late-socialist China, *Economy and Society*, 35(4): 550–70.

Hoffman, L.M. (2010) *Patriotic Professionalism in Urban China: Fostering Talent*, Philadelphia, PA: Temple University Press.

Holmes, M. (2004) Feeling beyond rules: politicizing the sociology of emotion and anger in feminist politics, *European Journal of Social Theory*, 7(2): 209–27.

Holmes, M. (2010) The emotionalization of reflexivity, *Sociology*, 44(1): 139–54.

Holmes, M. and McKenzie, J. (2018) Relational happiness through recognition and redistribution: emotion and inequality, *European Journal of Social Theory* 22(4): 439–57.

Howell, A. and Fan, C.C. (2011) Migration and inequality in Xinjiang: a survey of Han and Uyghur migrants in Urumqi, *Eurasian Geography and Economics*, 52(1): 119–39.

Howell, A., Ding, S. and Gustafsson, B.A. (2020) Investigating the patterns and determinants of Han and ethnic minority household migration in China, in B.A. Gustafsson, R. Hasmath and S. Ding (eds), *Ethnicity and Inequality in China*, Abingdon: Routledge, pp 259–82.

Hui, E.S.I. and Chan, C.K.C. (2022) From production to reproduction: pension strikes and changing characteristics of workers' collective action in China, *Journal of Industrial Relations*, 64(1): 3–25.

Iredale, R.R., Bilik, N., Su, W., Guo, F. and Hoy, C. (2001) *Contemporary Minority Migration, Education and Ethnicity in China*, Cheltenham and Northampton, MA: Edward Elgar.

Jacka, T. (2009) Cultivating citizens: suzhi (quality) discourse in the PRC, *Positions: East Asia Cultures Critique*, 17(3): 523–35.

Jacka, T. (2012) Migration, householding and the well-being of left-behind women in rural Ningxia, *China Journal*, 67: 1–21.

Jackson, S. and Scott, S. (2010) Rehabilitating interactionism for a feminist sociology of sexuality, *Sociology*, 44(5): 811–26.

Jamieson, L. (1999) Intimacy transformed? A critical look at the 'pure relationship', *Sociology*, 33(3): 477–94.

Jamieson, L. (2011) Intimacy as a concept: explaining social change in the context of globalisation or another form of ethnocentricism? *Sociological Research Online*, 16(4): 1–13.

Johnson, L. (2017) Bordering Shanghai: China's hukou system and processes of urban bordering, *Geoforum*, 80: 93–102.

Kang, M. (2003) The managed hand: the commercialization of bodies and emotions in Korean immigrant–owned nail salons, *Gender & Society*, 17(6): 820–39.

Kim, J. (2015) From 'country bumpkins' to 'tough workers': the pursuit of masculinity among male factory workers in China, *Anthropological Quarterly*, 88(1): 133.

Kipnis, A. (1997) *Producing Guanxi: Sentiment, Self, and Subculture in a North China Village*, Durham, NC, and London: Duke University Press.

Kipnis, A. (2006) Suzhi: a keyword approach, *The China Quarterly*, 186: 295–313.

Kipnis, A. (2007) Neoliberalism reified: suzhi discourse and tropes of neoliberalism in the People's Republic of China, *Journal of the Royal Anthropological Institute*, 13(2): 383–400.

Kleinman, A., Yunxiang, Y., Jun, J. and Lee, S. (eds) (2011) *Deep China: The Moral Life of the Person: What Anthropology and Psychiatry Tell Us about China Today*, Berkeley, CA: University of California Press.

Lee, C.K. (1998) *Gender and the South China Miracle: Two Worlds of Factory Women*, Berkeley, CA, and London: University of California Press.

Leibold, J. (2010) More than a category: Han supremacism on the Chinese internet, *The China Quarterly*, 203: 539–59.

REFERENCES

Leidner, R. (1991) Serving hamburgers and selling insurance: gender, work, and identity in interactive service jobs, *Gender & Society*, 5(2): 154–77.

Lerner, J., Rapoport, T. and Lomsky-Feder, E. (2007) The ethnic script in action: the regrounding of Russian Jewish immigrants in Israel, *Ethos*, 35(2): 168–95.

Li, J. (2003) Playing upon fantasy: women, ethnic tourism and the politics of identity construction in contemporary Xishuang Banna, China, *Tourism Recreation Research*, 28(2): 51–65.

Liang, Z. (2016) China's great migration and the prospects of a more integrated society, *Annual Review of Sociology*, 42(1): 451–71.

Liang, Z. and Ma, Z. (2014) Changing patterns of the floating population in China, 2000–2010, *Population and Development Review*, 40(4): 695–716.

Lin, J. and Mao, J. (2022a) Changing household registration and worker welfare in China and Vietnam, Policy Brief Series, Bielefeld: Bielefeld University.

Lin, J. and Mao, J. (2022b) Changing labour laws and worker welfare in Vietnam and China, Policy Brief Series, Bielefeld: Bielefeld University.

Lin, J. and Nguyen, M.T. (2021) The cycle of commodification: migrant labour, welfare, and the market in global China and Vietnam, *Global Public Policy and Governance*, 1(3): 321–39.

Lin, X. (2015) Rural–urban migration in China, in K. Ngok and C.K. Chan (eds), *China's Social Policy: Transformation and Challenges*, Abingdon: Routledge, pp 183–200.

Liu, J. (2016) *Gender, Sexuality and Power in Chinese Companies Beauties at Work*, London: Palgrave Macmillan.

Loveday, V. (2016) Embodying deficiency through 'affective practice': shame, relationality, and the lived experience of social class and gender in higher education, *Sociology*, 50(6): 1140–55.

Lui, L. (2016) Gender, rural–urban inequality, and intermarriage in China, *Social Forces*, 95(2): 639–62.

Lupton, D. (1998) *The Emotional Self: A Sociocultural Exploration*, London: Sage.

Ma, R. (2007) A new perspective in guiding ethnic relations in the 21st century: 'de-politicization' of ethnicity in China, *Asian Ethnicity*, 8: 199–217.

Ma, X. (2019) Ethnic minority empowerment and marginalization: Yi labour migrants outside China's Autonomous Regions, *China Information*, 33(2): 146–64.

Maccannell, D. (1973) Staged authenticity: arrangements of social space in tourist settings, *American Journal of Sociology*, 79(3): 589–603.

Made in China Journal (2017) National Bureau of Statistics Releases Annual Report on Migrant Workers. Available from: https://madeinchinajournal.com/2017/04/30/national-bureau-of-statistics-releases-annual-report-on-migrant-workers/ [Accessed 9 December 2019].

Mao, J. (2021) Bordering work and personal life: using 'the multiplication of labour' to understand ethnic performers' work in Southwest China, *China Perspectives*, 124: 9–18.

Mao, J. (2023a) Doing ethnicity: multi-layered ethnic scripts in contemporary China, *The China Quarterly*, 256: 1–15.

Mao, J. (2023b) Bringing emotional reflexivity and emotional regime to understanding 'the hukou puzzle' in contemporary China, *Emotions and Society*, (2023): 1–17.

Mao, J. and Yan, Z. (2023) 'Friends are those who can help you out': unpacking the understandings and experiences of friendships among young migrant workers in China, *Families, Relationships and Societies*, 1–17.

Mao, J., Nguyen, M. and Wilcox, P. (eds) (forthcoming) Special issue: rural futures in late socialist Asia: the countryside in a globalising world, *The Journal of Political Sociology*.

Mason, K. (2013) To your health! Toasting, intoxication and gendered critique among banqueting women, *China Journal*, 69: 108–33.

Maurer-Fazio, M., Hughes, J. and Zhang, D. (2007) An ocean formed from one hundred rivers: the effects of ethnicity, gender, marriage, and location on labor force participation in urban China, *Feminist Economics*, 13(3–4): 159–87.

Mavin, S. and Grandy, G. (2013) Doing gender well and differently in dirty work: the case of exotic dancing, *Gender, Work & Organization*, 20(3): 232–51.

May, V. (2011) *Sociology of Personal Life*, Basingstoke: Palgrave Macmillan.

McCall, L. (2005) The complexity of intersectionality, *Signs*, 30(3): 1771–800.

McCarthy, S.K. (2011) *Communist Multiculturalism Ethnic Revival in Southwest China*, Seattle, WA: University of Washington Press.

McKenzie, J. (2016) *Deconstructing Happiness: Critical Sociology and the Good Life*, New York and London: Routledge.

Mezzadra, S. and Neilson, B. (2013) *Border as Method, or the Multiplication of Labor*, Durham, NC and London: Duke University Press.

Mills, C.W. (2000) *The Sociological Imagination* (4th edn), Oxford: Oxford University Press.

Mullaney, T.S. (2011) *Coming to Terms with the Nation: Ethnic Classification in Modern China*, Berkeley, CA: University of California Press.

Murphy, R. (2002) *How Migrant Labor Is Changing Rural China*, Cambridge: Cambridge University Press.

Murphy, R. (2004) Turning peasants into modern Chinese citizens: 'Population quality' discourse, demographic transition and primary education, *The China Quarterly*, 177: 1–20.

Murphy, R. (2008) The impact of socio-cultural norms on women's experiences of migration and the implications for development, in *Migration and Development: Future Directions for Research and Policy*, SSRC Migration and Development Conference Papers, 28 February–1 March 2008, pp 256–76.

Muta, K. (2008) The making of Sekuhara: sexual harassment in Japanese culture, in S. Jackson, J. Liu and J. Woo (eds), *East Asian Sexualities: Modernity, Gender and New Sexual Cultures*, London: Zed Books, pp 52–68.

Nagel, J. (2000) Ethnicity and sexuality, *Annual Review of Sociology*, 26(1): 107–33.

Nash, K. (2009) *Contemporary Political Sociology: Globalization, Politics, and Power* (2nd edn), Chichester and Malden, MA: Wiley-Blackwell.

National Bureau of Statistics (2023) Statistical Bulletin of the People's Republic of China on National Economic and Social Development in 2022 (in Chinese). Available from: http://www.stats.gov.cn/ztjc/zthd/lhfw/2023/hgjj/202302/t20230228_1919000.html [Accessed 1 March 2023].

The National Law Review (2019) China responds to #MeToo; employers stay alert. Available from: https://www.natlawreview.com/article/china-responds-to-metoo-employers-stay-alert [Accessed 1 December 2019].

The New York Times (2018) 'Me Too', Chinese women say. not so fast, say the censors. Available from: https://www.nytimes.com/2018/01/23/world/asia/china-women-me-too-censorship.html [Accessed 20 December 2019].

Nyíri, P. (2006) *Scenic Spots: Chinese Tourism, the State, and Cultural Authority*, Seattle, WA, and London: University of Washington Press.

Nyíri, P. (2010) *Mobility and Cultural Authority in Contemporary China*, Seattle, WA: University of Washington Press.

Osburg, J. (2013) *Anxious Wealth: Money and Morality among China's New Rich*, Stanford, CA: Stanford University Press.

Otis, E. (2016) China's beauty proletariat: the body politics of hegemony in a Walmart cosmetics department, *Positions: East Asia Cultures Critique*, 24(1): 155.

Otis, E.M. (2011) *Markets and Bodies: Women, Service Work, and the Making of Inequality in China*, Stanford, CA: Stanford University Press.

Park, C.-H. (2014) Nongjiale tourism and contested space in rural China, *Modern China*, 40(5): 519–48.

People's Daily (2015) Xi's Yunnan visit highlights poverty elimination, ethnic solidarity, *People's Daily*, 22 January. Available from: http://en.people.cn/n/2015/0122/c90785-8839247.html [Accessed 20 November 2019].

Plamper, J. (2010) The history of emotions: an interview with Willian Reddy, Barbara Rosenwein, and Peter Stearns, *History and Theory*, 49(2): 237–65.

Pun, N. (2003) Subsumption or consumption? The phantom of consumer revolution in 'globalizing' China, *Cultural Anthropology*, 18(4): 469–92.

Pun, N. (2005) *Made in China: Women Factory Workers in a Global Workplace*, Hong Kong: Duke University Press.

Pun, N. (2016) *Migrant Labor in China: Post-Socialist Transformation*, Cambridge: Polity Press.

Pun, N. and Lu, H. (2010) Unfinished proletarianization: self, anger, and class action among the second generation of peasant-workers in present-day China, *Modern China*, 36(5): 493–519.

Rautio, S. (2021) Material compromises in the planning of a 'traditional village'in Southwest China, *Social Analysis*, 65(3): 67–87.

Reddy, W.M. (2001) *The Navigation of Feeling: A Framework for the History of Emotions*, Cambridge: Cambridge University Press.

Ridgeway, C.L. (2009) Framed before we know it: how gender shapes social relations, *Gender & Society*, 23(2): 145–60.

Ridgeway, C.L. (2011) *Framed by Gender: How Gender Inequality Persists in the Modern World*, New York and Oxford: Oxford University Press.

Rippa, A. (2020) *Borderland Infrastructures: Trade, Development, and Control in Western China*, Amsterdam: Amsterdam University Press.

Robinson, J. (2013) *Ordinary Cities: Between Modernity and Development*, London: Routledge.

Rofel, L. (2007) *Desiring China: Experiments in Neoliberalism, Sexuality, and Public Culture*, Durham, NC, and London: Duke University Press.

Rose, N. (1992) Governing the enterprising self, in P. Heelas and P. Morris (eds), *The Values of the Enterprise Culture: The Moral Debate*, London: Routledge, pp 141–64.

Ross, B.L. (2000) Bumping and grinding on the line: making nudity pay, *Labour/Le Travail*, 46: 221–50.

Said, E.W. (1978) Orientalism, New York: Pantheon Books.

Salazar, N.B. and Schiller, N.G. (eds) (2014) *Regimes of Mobility: Imaginaries and Relationalities of Power*, London: Routledge.

Salzinger, L. (2004) Revealing the unmarked: finding masculinity in a global factory, *Ethnography*, 5(1): 5–27.

Schein, L. (1997) Gender and internal orientalism in China, *Modern China*, 23(1): 69–98.

Schein, L. (2000) *Minority Rules: The Miao and the Feminine in China's Cultural Politics*, Durham, NC: Duke University Press.

Schein, L. (2006) Negotiating scale: Miao women at a distance, in T. Oakes and L. Schein (eds), *Translocal China: Linkages, Identities and the Reimagining of Space*, Abingdon: Routledge, pp 213–37.

Shen, Y. (2019) *Beyond Tears and Laughter: Gender, Migration, and the Service Sector in China*, Singapore: Palgrave Macmillan.

Shi, S.-J. (2006) Left to market and family – again? Ideas and the development of the rural pension policy in china, *Social Policy & Administration*, 40(7): 791–806.

Shi, S.-J. (2012) Towards inclusive social citizenship? Rethinking China's social security in the trend towards urban–rural harmonization, *Journal of Social Policy*, 41(4): 789–810.

Shi, S.-J. (2017) Social decentralization: exploring the competitive solidarity of regional social protection in China, *Journal of Asian Public Policy*, 10(1): 74–89.

Simon, W. and Gagnon, J. (1986) Sexual scripts: permanence and change, *Archives of Sexual Behavior*, 15(2): 97–120.

Skeggs, B. (1997) *Formations of Class and Gender: Becoming Respectable*, London: Sage.

Skeggs, B. (2004) *Class, Self, Culture*, London: Routledge.

Skeggs, B. (2011) Imagining personhood differently: person value and autonomist working-class value practices, *The Sociological Review*, 59(3): 496–513.

Smart, C. (2007) *Personal Life: New Directions in Sociological Thinking*, Oxford: Polity Press.

Solinger, D.J. (1999) *Contesting Citizenship in Urban China: Peasant Migrants, the State, and the Logic of the Market*, Berkeley, CA, and London: University of California Press.

State Council (2014) Opinions on further promoting reforms of the hukou system. Guofa [2014] No. 25.

Su, Y., Tesfazion, P. and Zhao, Z. (2018) Where are the migrants from? Inter- vs. intra-provincial rural–urban migration in China, *China Economic Review*, 47: 142–55.

Sun, W. (2009) Suzhi on the move: body, place, and power, *Positions: East Asia Cultures Critique*, 17(3): 617–42.

Sun, W. (2013) Inequality and culture: a new pathway to understanding social inequality, in W. Sun and Y. Guo (eds), *Unequal China: The Political Economy and Cultural Politics of Inequality*, Abingdon: Routledge, pp 43–58.

Sun, W. (2023) *Love Troubles: Inequality in China and Its Intimate Consequences*, London: Bloomsbury Publishing.

Svašek, M. and Skrbiš, Z. (2007) Passions and powers: emotions and globalization, *Identities: Emotions and Globalisation*, 14(4): 367–83.

Swider, S. (2017) Informal and precarious work: he precariat and China, *Rural China*, 14(1): 19–41.

Tao, R. (2010) Achieving real progress in China's hukou reform, *East Asia Forum*, 8 February.

Tao, R. and Xu, Z. (2007) Urbanization, rural land system and social security for migrants in China, *The Journal of Development Studies*, 43(7): 1301–20.

Tian, X. and Deng, Y. (2017) Organizational hierarchy, deprived masculinity, and confrontational practices: men doing women's jobs in a global factory, *Journal of Contemporary Ethnography*, 46(4): 464–89.

Uretsky, E. (2016) *Occupational Hazards: Business, Sex, and HIV in Post-Mao China*, Redwood City, CA: Stanford University Press.

Urry, J. (2002) *The Tourist Gaze* (2nd edn), London: Sage.

Walsh, E.R. (2001) The Mosuo: beyond the myths of matriarchy: gender transformation and economic development, Temple University, ProQuest Dissertations and Theses.

Walsh, E.R. (2005) From Nü Guo to Nü'er Guo: negotiating desire in the land of the Mosuo, *Modern China*, 31(4): 448–86.

Walsh, E.R. and Swain, M.B. (2004) Creating modernity by touring paradise: domestic ethnic tourism in Yunnan, China, *Tourism Recreation Research*, 29(2): 59–68.

Wang, X. and Nehring, D. (2014) Individualization as an ambition: mapping the dating landscape in Beijing, *Modern China*, 40(6): 578–604.

Wang, Y., Hu, Z., Peng, K., Xin, Y., Yang, Y., Drescher, J. et al (2019) Discrimination against LGBT populations in China, *The Lancet Public Health*, 4(9): e440-1.

Warhurst, C. and Nickson, D. (2009) 'Who's got the look?' Emotional, aesthetic and sexualized labour in interactive services, *Gender, Work & Organization*, 16(3): 385–404.

Weeks, K. (2007) Life within and against work: affective labor, feminist critique, and post-Fordist politics, *Ephemera: Theory and Politics in Organization*, 7(1): 233–49.

West, C. and Zimmerman, D.H. (1987) Doing gender, *Gender & Society*, 1(2): 125–51.

Wettergren, A. (2009) Fun and laughter: culture jamming and the emotional regime of late capitalism, *Social Movement Studies*, 8(1): 1.

Wettergren, A. (2010) Managing unlawful feelings: the emotional regime of the Swedish migration board, *International Journal of Work Organisation and Emotion*, 3(4): 400–19.

Whats on Weibo (2019) Chinese netizens discuss: 'Do you say "Thank you" to the food delivery man?' Available from: https://www.whatsonweibo.com/chinese-netizens-quarrel-do-you-say-thank-you-to-the-food-delivery-man/ [Accessed 20 November 2019].

Wielander, G. (2018) Happiness in Chinese socialist discourse – Ah Q and the 'visible hand', in G. Wielander and D. Hird (eds), *Chinese Discourses on Happiness*, Hong Kong: Hong Kong University Press, pp 25–43.

Wielander, G. and Hird, D. (2018) *Chinese Discourses on Happiness*, Hong Kong: Hong Kong University Press.

Wilcox, E.E. (2016) Beyond internal Orientalism: dance and nationality discourse in the early People's Republic of China, 1949–1954, *The Journal of Asian Studies*, 75(2): 363–86.

Wingfield, A.H. (2010) Are some emotions marked "whites only"? Racialized feeling rules in professional workplaces, *Social Problems*, 57(2): 251–68.

Witz, A., Warhurst, C. and Nickson, D. (2003) The labour of aesthetics and the aesthetics of organization, *Organization*, 10(1): 33–54.

REFERENCES

Woodman, S. (2017) Legitimating exclusion and inclusion: 'culture', education and entitlement to local urban citizenship in Tianjin and Lanzhou, *Citizenship Studies: Practicing Citizenship in Contemporary China*, 21(7): 755–72.

Woodman, S. (2018) All citizenship is local, in C.M. Lyon and A.F. Goebel (eds), *Citizenship and Place: Case Studies on the Borders of Citizenship*, Londonand Lanham, MD: Rowman & Littlefield.

Woodman, S. (2019) The cultural politics of women's human rights in transnational China, in G. Wu, Y. Feng and H. Lansdowne (eds), *Gender Dynamics, Feminist Activism and Social Transformation in China*, Abingdon and New York: Routledge.

Woodman, S. and Guo, Z. (2017) Introduction: practicing citizenship in contemporary China, *Citizenship Studies: Practicing Citizenship in Contemporary China*, 21(7): 737–54.

Xiang, B. (2021) Suspension: seeking agency for change in the hypermobile world, *Pacific Affairs*, 94(2): 233–50.

Xie, K. (2021) *Embodying Middle Class Gender Aspirations: Perspectives from China's Privileged Young Women*, Singapore: Palgrave Macmillan.

Yan, H. (2003) Neoliberal governmentality and neohumanism: organizing suzhi/value flow through labor recruitment networks, *Cultural Anthropology*, 18(4): 493–523.

Yan, Y. (2003) *Private Life under Socialism Love, Intimacy, and Family Change in a Chinese Village, 1949–1999*, Stanford, CA: Stanford University Press.

Yan, Y. (2010) The Chinese path to individualization, *British Journal of Sociology*, 61(3): 489–512.

Yang, J. (ed.) (2014) *The Political Economy of Affect and Emotion in East Asia*, London and New York: Routledge.

Yang, L. (2011) Ethnic tourism and cultural representation, *Annals of Tourism Research*, 38(2): 561–85.

Yang, L. and Wall, G. (2008) Ethnic tourism development: Chinese government perspectives, *Annals of Tourism Research*, 35(3): 751–71.

Yi, L. (2005) Choosing between ethnic and Chinese citizenship: the educational trajectories of Tibetan minority children in Northwestern China, in V.L. Fong and R. Murphy (eds), *Chinese Citizenship: Views from the Margins*, London and New York: Routledge, pp 41–67.

Yi, L. (2011) Turning rurality into modernity: suzhi education in a suburban public school of migrant children in Xiamen, *The China Quarterly*, 206: 313–30.

Yuval-Davis, N. (2013) A situated intersectional everyday approach to the study of bordering, *Euborderscapes Working Paper*, 2.

Zang, X. (2015) *Ethnicity in China: A Critical Introduction*, Cambridge: Polity Press.

Zelizer, V.A. (2000) The purchase of intimacy, *Law & Social Inquiry*, 25(3): 817–48.

Zhang, C. (2018) Governing neoliberal authoritarian citizenship: theorizing hukou and the changing mobility regime in China, *Citizenship Studies*, 22(8): 855–81.

Zhang, L. (2021) Contextualizing precarious work: labor dispatch, boundary-drawing, and the politics of labor regulation in post-socialist China, *Labor History*, 62(5–6): 556–74.

Zheng, T. (2003) Consumption, body image, and rural–urban apartheid in contemporary China, *City & Society*, 15(2): 143–63.

Zheng, T. (2006) Cool masculinity: male clients' sex consumption and business alliance in urban China's sex industry, *Journal of Contemporary China*, 15(46): 161–82.

Zheng, T. (2007) Performing media-constructed images for first-class citizenship: political struggles of rural migrant hostesses in Dalian, *Critical Asian Studies*, 39(1): 89–120.

Zhou, M., Murphy, R. and Tao, R. (2014) Effects of parents' migration on the education of children left behind in rural China, *Population and Development Review*, 40(2): 273–92.

Zhou, Y., Lin, G.C., and Zhang, J. (2019) Urban China through the lens of neoliberalism: is a conceptual twist enough? *Urban Studies*, 56(1): 33–43.

Index

References to figures appear in *italic* type.

A

accents 71
aesthetic labour 34, 108–9
　connection with sexualized labour 109
affective labour at banqueting table 33–6
African drummers 93
Ahmed, S. 11, 52, 64, 87
anger 65, 86, 96, 115
'ascribed minorities' 78, 80
'aspirational urbanism' 71
austerity campaign 35, 110

B

Bai, Z. 10, 11, 76, 123, 127, 128
Bai people 10–11
bancan (accompanying meals) 19, 25, 28–30, 29, 105–6, 108
　bodily contact in 29, 35, 104, 116
　in context of banqueting and business entertainment customs 34–5
　doing affective labour at banqueting table 33–6
　doing 'distinction work' and creating intimacy 108–11
　as interactive service work 25, 33, 50, 104, 123
　working conditions 42–3
banqueting customs 34–5
Barabantseva, E. 36, 69, 74, 93
Beck, U. 14, 128
Bentley, G.C. 80
bill-paying practices 48
bodies
　ethnicized 70–1, 94, 103
　as markers of otherness 11–12
border encounters 2
　intimate 25, 43–9, *45*, 50, 123–6
　　desires to be respectable and modern 46–9, 124–5
　　entitlement to respect 43–6, 49
　through migration and work 11–12

bordering processes 2, 12, 25, 40–3, 124–5
Bourdieu, P. 80
Burkitt, I. 53, 58, 60, 129
business entertainment customs 34–5

C

capital, expansion of frontier of 40–3
Chang, L.T. 43
Chen, C. 5, 22, 52, 54, 55, 57, 61, 124
China Dream 51, 64
Choi, S.Y. 7, 13, 48, 53, 59, 88, 114, 117, 119, 120
class 37, 41, 86, 88, 130
　gender and making distinctions of 108
　hukou contributing to formation of 54
　and sense of entitlement 45, 59
consumer revolution 9
costumes 19, 26, 38, 75
　changing out of 38, 46
　deposits for 102
cultural aspects of rural-urban divide 52, 66–72, 73, 124–5
　desire, value and project of self 66–70
　encountering rural–urban borders everyday 70–2
cultural authority of the state
　around mobility 69, 70
　bordering processes working through 125
　in tourism 31–2, 40–1
cultural politics of inequality 130–1
'cultural scenarios' 82, 97
customers
　entertaining VIP 30, 108–11
　ethnic performers pretending to be 'authentic' for 39, 70, 81
　female performers sitting on laps of male 30, 34, 39, 109, 112–13, 118
　gendered interactions with 115
　lack of respect for and poor treatment of ethnic performers 44–5
　power over ethnic performers 36, 43, 47

147

questions about, and views on, ethnic minorities 5, 32, 38, 70–1
responding to sexual attention and harassment from male 106–7
'service encounters' with 11–12, 15, 37, 104, 123

D

Dai people 11, 89
dating 48, 119–20
deposit money 42, 102–3
'differential' inclusion of migrants 3, 36, 41, 103, 124
'distinction work' 37, 108, 126, 128
drinking
  compulsory 27–8, 29, 34–5, 89, 113
  cross-cupped wine 29, 30, 104, 116

E

economic gap 6, 44
economic growth 9, 18, 110
emotion work 86–8, 97, 115
emotional gap 44–6
emotional labour 33, 35, 76, 86
  gendered ways of doing 115, 120
emotional politics of ethnicity 85–9
emotional reflexivity
  defining 58
  in making *hukou* transfer decisions 23, 58–63, 129
emotional regime 63, 124, 129
  intersection with migration regime 63–6, 72–3
emotions 15, 52, 129
  positive and negative 64–5, 96, 124
  in theorizing rural–urban migration 52–4, 129
employment, precarious 41–3
'enterprising self' 16, 88, 92, 95, 97, 116
entertainment after work 46–9
entitlement, sense of
  to *hukou* 59
  to respect 43–6, 49, 88
entitlement, structures of 45–6, 59
ethnic assessment 23, 76, 80, 81
Ethnic Classification Project 6
'ethnic folk villages' (*minzu cun*) 8, 40
ethnic minorities
  'ascribed minorities' 78, 103
  avoiding shame 68
  binary distinction between Han and 83
  classification project 75
  customer questions about, and views on 5, 32, 38, 70–1
  as ethnic Others 9, 11–12, 38, 83
  ethnic performers and identifying as 32, 38–9, 77–8
  ethnic performers portraying imagined 69–70
  groups 2, 5, 6, 74
  localization of 69
  marginalizing and excluding of 32–3
  representations of 6, 32, 68, 83, 85
    textbook depictions 81, 89
    women 83–4, 105–6
  ronghe ideology of state towards 79, 84
  rural–urban migrants from 6–7
  suzhi of 16, 64, 94, 103
  younger generation 5–6
ethnic performance (*minzu biaoyan*) 1, 22–3, 25–50, 123–4
  commercialization of intimacy 109–10
  emergence of commercialized 9–10
  flourishing in austerity campaign 35, 110
  'framed by ethnicity' 37–8, 75–6, 80
  gendered division of labour 116, 120
  Han taking over 32–3
  multi-layered meaning 30–6
    doing affective labour at banqueting table 33–6
    performing ethnicity under cultural authority of state 30–3
  prevalence 8–12
  reframing meaning of 94–5
  as sexualized labour 104–8, 120, 125–6
  ethnic scripts and legitimizing 111–14, 126
  as a site of encounters 23, 25, 36–43, 50, 123–4
    bordering processes 40–3
    encountering ethnicity, gender and rural-urban divide 37–40
  stage performances 28, 29, 108, 116
  work 26–30
  see also bancan (accompanying meals)
ethnic performers 2, 5
  ambivalence towards own identity 75, 77–8, 81, 88, 129
  blurred boundaries between work and personal lives 17, 49, 86, 109, 127
  cultivating skills 90–1, 116
  customer power over 36, 43, 47
  'differential' inclusion of migrant 3, 36, 41, 103, 124
  encountering ethnicity in daily work 75–8, 125
  encountering rural–urban border everyday 70–2
  ethnicity as 'doing' rather than 'being' 78–81, 97, 125
  Han people taking over from minority people as 32–3
  identifying as genuine ethnic minorities 32
  identifying as not from 'authentic' ethnic minorities 32, 38–9, 77–8
  intimate border encounters 25, 43–9, *45*, 50, 123–6
    desires to be respectable and modern 46–9, 124–5
    sense of entitlement to respect 43–6, 49

INDEX

intimate negotiations with significant
  others 117–20
motivations for becoming 1–2
off-work consumption and
  entertainment 46–9
portraying imagined ethnic minority 69–70
pretending to be 'authentic' for
  customers 39, 70, 81
researching 'untypical migrants' 3–8
'service encounters' with customers 11–12,
  15, 37, 104, 123
unique form of service work 7–8
working as 26–30
working conditions 26–7, 41–3
ethnic performers, female
  doing 'distinction work' and creating
    intimacy at banqueting tables 108–11
  expressing negative emotions 96
  intimate negotiations with significant
    others 117–19, 121
  'out-of-placeness' 99–104
  participating in after work
    entertainment 48–9
  scrutiny of 'virtuous reputations' of 100–1,
    103, 111, 119, 120, 126
  sexualized labour 104–8, 120
    struggles and resistance in response to
      sexualized labour 111–14, 116
  sitting on laps of male customers 30, 34,
    39, 109, 112–13, 118
ethnic performers, male
  career paths and future plans 116
  intimate negotiations with significant
    others 119–20
  masculine compromise at work 114–17,
    120–1
  off-work consumption and
    entertainment 47–8
  sexualized labour 116–17, 120, 126
ethnic scripts 80, 125
  'authentic' ethnicity of 88–9, 91, 97
  in context of Southwest China 85
  dangerous ethnic practices 84
  for distinct groups 85
  emotional politics of ethnicity 85–9
  legitimizing sexualization of ethnic
    performance 111–14, 126
  multi-layered meaning 81–5, 113–14
  sexualizing minority women 83–4, 105–6
  state promotion of scripts 84, 97
ethnic self, cultivating 85–96
  cultivating talents and 89–96
  emotional politics of ethnicity 85–9
ethnic tourism 8–9, 10–11, 40
  boosting local economy 18, 40–1
  cultural authority of the state 31–2, 40–1
  as a daily reminder of ethnicity 7–8, 10–11,
    76–7, 123
  and portrayal of minority women 83–4

poverty alleviation through engaging
  with 18, 89–90, 111
see also restaurants, rural tourism
ethnicity
  ambivalence towards 75, 77–8, 81, 88, 129
  cultivating ethnic-self 85–96
    cultivating talents and 89–96
    emotional politics of ethnicity 85–9
  embodied elements of 70–1
  emotional politics of 85–9
  encountering 13, 23, 74–81
    in daily work 75–8, 125
    as 'doing' rather than 'being' 78–81,
      97, 125
  ethnic performance 'framed' by 37–8,
    75–6, 80
  ethnic scripts 81–5
    overriding people's experiences of
      ethnicity 88–9, 91, 97
  ethnic tourism and commercialization
    of 89–90
  ethnic tourism as a daily reminder of 7–8,
    10–11, 76–7, 123
  labour market and 7
  in migration studies 6–7
  minzu, meaning of 74–5
  minzu classifications 75
  performing ethnicity under cultural
    authority of state 30–3

F

Factory Girls (Chang) 44
factory work 4, 7, 33, 41, 42, 92, 102, 114
Fan, C.C. 5, 6, 22, 52, 54, 55, 57, 61, 124
feeling rules 86–7, 97, 125
feminist activism 101, 107, 126
Feminist Five 107
financial capability 48, 88
Forest Park 19, 29, 83
  bancan 29–30, 29
  introduction from host 32, 39, 105–6
  VIP clients 109

G

Gagnon, J. 81, 82
Gaudette, R. 93
gender
  in construction of 'distinction work' 37,
    108, 126, 128
  'doing' 80, 81
  encounters framed by 37–8, 39
  intersecting with race and class 86
gendering of border struggles 23–4, 99–121
  intimate negotiations with significant
    others 117–20, 121
  masculine compromise at work 114–17
  'out-of-placeness' 99–104
  undertaking sexualized labour 104–14
Giddens, A. 14, 58

149

'Green City' 1, 4
  ethnic groups 74
  flourishing ethnic tourism 40–1, 89–90
  hukou 56–7, 60–1, 62, 102, 124
  research sites 4, 18–19
Grillot, C. 12, 34
guanxi-building 34–5, 39, 109–10
guests *see* customers

H

habitus 80
Han 5
  assimilation project 79
  binary distinction between ethnic minorities and 83
  'gaze' 30–1, *31*, 39
  taking over ethnic performance work 32–3
Hani people 5, 76, 77, 78, 103
Hanser, A. 7, 11, 23, 37, 45, 59, 108, 123, 126
happiness, discourse of 15, 64
'happiness duty' 64, 87
hegemonic masculinity 59, 88, 96, 117, 126
Hochschild, A.R. 3, 33, 34, 36, 86, 91, 125, 127, 128
Hoffman, L. 16, 67, 95
Holmes, M. 53, 58, 60, 64, 65
home-place-identity 62
hukou 3–4, 54–66
  access to social welfare 102
  being out-of-place in system 101–4
  emotional reflexivity in making *hukou* transfer decisions 23, 58–63, 129
  encountering rural–urban bordering through 12, 41, 54–66, 124
  and home-place-identity construction 62
  intersection between emotional regime and migration regime 63–6, 72–3
  land entitlement issues 60–2
  opaque system 57, 60
  point-based systems for *hukou* transfer 56–7
  policy in Green City 56–7, 60
  'puzzle' 22, 52, 54–6, 72, 124
  recent reforms 4–5, 56–7
  sense of entitlement to 59

I

individualization process 14, 16, 128
inequality, cultural politics of 130–1
intersectionality 129–30
interviews with informants 21–2
intimacy
  commercialization of 109–10
  creating intimacy at banqueting tables 108–11
  as a lens 2, 13–17, 122–3, 127–31
  sociology of 13, 14–15
  using affective labour to facilitate 36
intimate border encounters 25, 43–9, *45*, 50, 123–6

  desires to be respectable and modern 46–9, 124–5
  entitlement to respect 43–6, 49
  intimate negotiations with significant others 117–20, 121
'intra-category' positioning 129

K

Kang, M. 86, 104
karaoke clubs 35, 46, 110

L

labour
  intersection of mobility, capital and 40–3
  laws 42
  market 7–8
  multiplication of 50, 76, 114, 127–8
Lahu 67–8, 84, 87, 90
  recruiting 94
  songs 10, 87, 90
  villages 40, 84
land, entitlement to 60–2
leave time, taking 42–3
Lerner, J. 82
Li, J. 10, 11, 77, 128
Liu, J. 101, 111, 117
localization 69

M

Mao, J. 4, 12, 15, 35, 42, 54, 73, 80, 98, 102, 114
marriage
  avoiding an arranged 102, 103
  postponing 102
  proposing 10
  undesirable partners 48, 117, 119, 126
  women's prospects for a good 100, 126
masculine compromise at work 114–17, 120–1
massages, shoulder 27–8, 106, 116
May, V. 13, 14, 17, 127
McCarthy, S.K. 9, 84, 95
McKenzie, J. 53, 64
medical insurance 102
men
  dating 48, 119–20
  hegemonic masculinity 59, 88, 96, 117, 126
  marriage prospects for migrant 48, 117, 119, 126
  masculine compromise at work 114–17, 120–1
  see also ethnic performers, male
methods *see* research methods
#MeToo movement 107
Mezzadra, S. 12, 23, 36, 40, 41, 52, 53, 76, 103, 114, 123, 127, 128
Miao women 105
migrants *see* ethnic performers; ethnic performers, female; ethnic performers, male; rural–urban migrants

INDEX

migration
  being modern through embracing 66–70
  border encounters through work and 11–12
  emotions in theorizing rural–urban 52–4, 129
  regime intersection with emotional regime 63–6, 72–3
minzu
  classification project 75
  meaning 74–5
  see also ethnicity
mobile phones 110, 111
mobility
  associations with immorality 100–1
  and becoming modern citizens 67–70
  cultural authority of the state regarding 69, 70
  different forms of 37, 41
  hukou problematizing 59–60, 103
  intersection of labour, capital and 40–3
  self-development, self-improvement and 92–3
modern
  desire to become respectable and 46–9
  embracing migration to be 66–70
modernization process 69
Mosuo people 83–4
multiplication of labour 50, 76, 114, 127–8

N

nail salons, workers in 86, 104
Nash, K. 130
Neilson, B. 12, 23, 36, 40, 41, 52, 53, 76, 103, 114, 123, 127, 128
neoliberal ideology 16, 63–4, 67, 124, 130
Nyíri, P. 4, 9, 25, 31, 40, 69, 70, 125

O

off-work consumption and entertainment 46–9
'on-stage' and 'off-stage' self 11, 77, 128
the Other 9, 11–12, 38, 83
Otis, E. 7, 42, 43, 46, 71, 100, 105, 106, 109
'out-of-placeness' 99–104, 125

P

participant observation 20–1
Peng, Y. 7, 13, 48, 53, 59, 88, 114, 117, 119, 120
pension schemes 61
personal life
  blurred boundaries between work and 17, 49, 86, 109, 127
  negotiating impact of work on 117–20
  in public space 17
  sociology of personal life approach 13–14, 15, 127
personhood 15–17, 128
  achieving valuable 52, 90, 91, 95, 125, 128–9
poverty, escaping 8, 9, 18, 40, 90, 111

power relations in service encounters 36, 43, 47
project of the self 66–7, 70

R

race and feeling rules 86
racialized sexualization 104
Reddy, W.M. 15, 53, 54, 63, 124
religious practices 84
research methods 17–22
  choice of research sites 4, 18–19
  gaining access to research sites 19
  informant interviews 21–2
  participant observation 20–1
respect, sense of entitlement to 43–6, 49, 88
restaurants, rural tourism
  ethnic performance 1–2, 9
  sites of research 18–20
  see also Forest Park; Tea Park; Waterfall Restaurant
Ridgeway, C.L. 25, 37, 38, 39
ronghe ideology 79, 84
Rose, N. 16, 49, 66–7, 86, 88, 92, 95
Ross, B.L. 117
rural femininity 119
rural tourism restaurants *see* restaurants, rural tourism
rural–urban divide
  bordering through *hukou* 12, 41, 54–66, 124
  cultural aspect 52, 66–72, 73, 124–5
  desire, value and project of self 66–70
  encountering rural–urban borders everyday 70–2
  ethnic performance as a site of encounter shaped by 40
  gendered bordering process of 99–104
rural–urban migrants
  'differential' inclusion 3, 36, 41, 103, 124
  emotions in theorizing 52–4, 129
  from ethnic minorities 6–7
  as an example of individualization process 16
  fulfilling China Dream 51
  intra-provincial migrants 2, 4, 22, 122
  literature gaps 4
  motivations to migrate 3, 45, 51–2, 102
  numbers 3
  precarious employment 41–3
  suzhi of 16, 64, 94, 103
  see also ethnic performers; ethnic performers, female; ethnic performers, male

S

Said, E.W. 9
Schein, L. 9, 10, 31, 39, 83, 98, 105, 120
self
  -development, self-improvement and, mobility 92–3

'enterprising' 16, 88, 92, 95, 97, 116
  -making 15–16, 128
'on-stage' and 'off-stage' 11, 77, 128
project of the 66–7, 70
  see also ethnic self, cultivating
service work 5, 7
  encounters with customers 11–12, 15, 37, 104, 123
  as a form of encounter 37
  growth of sector 9
  interactive 25, 33, 50, 104, 123
  masculinities challenged in 114–15
sex, industry 110
sex culture 101, 103, 119
sex workers 12, 105
sexual harassment 106–8
sexual scripts 81, 82, 84
sexuality
  moralizing of women's 48–9, 100–1, 103, 111, 119, 120, 126
  politics of 110
  portrayals of ethnic minority women's 83–4, 105–6
sexualized labour 34, 39, 104–14, 125–6
  connection with aesthetic labour 109
  doing 'distinction work' and creating intimacy at banqueting tables 108–11
  ethnic performance as 104–8, 120, 125–6
  and impact on intimate relationships 117–20, 121
  of men 116–17, 120, 126
  struggles and resistance in response to 111–14
Shenzhen 4
shows 28, 29, 108, 116
Simon, W. 81, 82
site of encounter, ethnic performance as 23, 25, 36–43, 50, 123–4
  bordering processes 40–3
  encountering ethnicity, gender and rural-urban divide 37–40
Skeggs, B. 14, 16–17, 20, 45, 49, 90, 95, 125
Smart, C. 13, 14, 127
social welfare 102
songs 10, 33, 90–1, 106
  'If you are going to visit me tonight' 39
  Lahu 10, 87, 90
Spring Festival Gala 8
stage performances 28, 29, 108, 116
strikes 32–3, 42
'structures of entitlement' 45–6, 59
suzhi (human quality) 16, 63–4, 69, 70, 71, 83
  low 16, 64, 94, 103

T

Tea Park 19, 28
  daily suzhi training 70

recruiting "the right bodies" 94
working as an ethnic performer in 28–9
therapeutic governance 15
toasting 34, 109, 111
  avoiding rounds of 113
tourism see ethnic tourism
'tourist gaze' 30, 32, 33
tourists' mobility 41

U

Urry, J. 30, 32, 33

V

value, subject of 16–17
Vietnamese sex workers 12

W

Wa people 32, 83, 89, 94–5
Wall, G. 9, 10
Waterfall Restaurant 19, 26
  deposit money 42, 102–3
  ensuring privacy of guests 110–11
  strike by ethnic performers 32–3
  working as an ethnic performer in 26–8, 27
  working conditions 26, 42–3
Weeks, K. 49, 127
West, C. 80, 81
Wettergren, A. 63
Wingfield, A.H. 86
women
  eroticized representations of ethnic minority 83–4, 105–6
  rural 101, 103, 105, 119
  scrutiny of 'virtuous reputations' of 48–9, 100–1, 103, 111, 119, 120, 126
  see also ethnic performers, female
working conditions 26–7, 41–3

X

Xi Jinping 18, 35, 51, 110

Y

Yan, H. 16, 64
Yan, Y. 16
Yang, J. 15, 63, 64, 67
Yang, L. 8, 9, 10
yanzhi (appearance value) 34, 108–9
Yao people 36
Yunnan Province 4, 18, 31–2
  ethnic minority groups 74
  tourism 76, 105

Z

Zelizer, V.A. 109
Zhang, C. 5, 56
Zhang, J. 12, 34
Zimmerman, D.H. 80, 81